Dewey® & the Decimals

Learning Games & Activities

Paige Taylor and
Kent and Sue Brinkmeyer

Alleyside
Press®

Fort Atkinson, Wisconsin

Acknowledgments

The authors wish to express their gratitude to the several teachers who "road tested" the activities in this book, including Jean Pulone, Rose Ryland, Lynne Holl, Kathy Thomas, and Kathyrn Bikle of Barnhart School in Arcadia, CA; Jeanne Culbertson of Chaparral Elementary School, Claremont, CA; Tracy Little of Ranch Hills Elementary School, Pomona, CA; Robin Enos of Elliott Point Elementary School, Ft. Walton Beach, FL; and Judy Mau of Mesa Robles School, Hacienda Heights, CA.

In addition, we are grateful to the following librarians for their input: Donna Watkins and her staff of the Pasadena (CA) City Library (Hastings Branch) and Violet Kuroki and Estelle Ichino, catalogers with the Los Angeles Public Library.

Last, appreciation goes to Brownie Troop 172, Mt. Wilson Vista Council (Arcadia, CA); Charlotte Taylor, Leslie Howard, Lauren Schenker and Michelle Yellin for their creative ideas, and to Paul Schenker and Susan Miles for their patient technical assistance.

Published by **Alleyside Press**

An imprint of Highsmith Press LLC

W5527 Highway 106

P.O. Box 800

Fort Atkinson, Wisconsin 53538-0800

1-800-558-2110

Library of Congress Cataloging-in-Publication Data

Taylor, Paige.

   Dewey & the decimals : learning games & activities / by Paige Taylor, Kent Brinkmeyer, and Sue Brinkmeyer.

    p. cm.

   ISBN 1-57950-050-1 (alk. paper)

   1. Classification, Dewey decimal--Problems, exercises, etc. 2. Elementary school libraries--Activity programs. I. Title: Dewey and the decimals. II. Brinkmeyer, Kent. III. Brinkmeyer, Sue. IV. Title.

  Z696.D7 T39 2001

  025.4'31--dc21

                   2001002278

Contents

6. Computer and On-line Catalogs

Appendix A

Appendix B

Appendix C

Introduction

We are in the Information Age. Just considering children's books alone, approximately four thousand are published in the U.S. each year and a leading Internet bookseller has one hundred thousand titles available for purchase! A major challenge for youth, as for adults, is to keep pace with the vast amount of information available through books and audio-visual media. Key to that process is understanding how resources are organized in libraries.

The main focus of this activity book is on teaching elementary students how to use the Dewey Decimal Classification® System (DDC), which remains the most widely utilized method of arranging library books in the United States. The version of the DDC on which the book is based is the 13th Edition (Abridged), which is the newest and most commonly used by schools and libraries.

A book for librarians and teachers

The book is intended equally for librarians and teachers. School librarians may wish to use the activities as the basis for (or adjuncts to) their school curriculum. Public librarians can create after-school and summer library programs from the contents. Teachers will find the activities valuable as the foundation for library unit lesson plans (or for reinforcement of information learned on library visits), and for study skills classes preparing students to do research. The games also make constructive rainy day activities and hip-pocket lesson plans for library aides, teachers and substitutes.

Goals and objectives

Students will be able to progressively acquire skills that will prepare them for accessing information throughout school and adult life. They will learn the basic structure of the Dewey Decimal Classification System and how to use the computer catalog to find all types of nonfiction, including reference works and audio-visual materials. Information on using the Internet is woven into applicable exercises. A major objective of the book is to provide students with tools for doing research and encourage them to go beyond the encyclopedia.

How to use this book

Activities and worksheets are included for each skill and are labeled according to grade level. Very basic activities such as grouping, numbering, and simple alphabetization are included for the youngest students while more advanced exercises, such as working with decimals and the computer catalog, are designed for older students. Specifically, activities are designed to teach the following skills:

PreK–K: Recognition and ordering of numbers 0–9; recognition of authors' last names and titles of books; basic grouping of like subjects; general knowledge of fiction and nonfiction.

Grades 1–2: Recognition and ordering of numbers 0–99; simple alphabetization of authors (by first letter of last names only); general understanding of differences between fiction and nonfiction; awareness of groupings by subject of nonfiction.

Grades 3–4: Recognition and ordering of numbers 0–999, with general introduction to decimals; categorization of books as fiction and nonfiction (including biographies and reference books); introduction to using computer catalog.

Grades 5–6: Recognition and ordering of all numbers using decimals; working knowledge of Dewey classifications; ability to locate books using computer catalog (independently or with minimal assistance from librarians); ability to use the Internet in conjunction with the computer catalog, and familiarity with Boolean terms.

Recommended sequences by grade level are included on pages ___ for further assistance in mapping out lessons.

A variety of activities are presented for each skill, and include games, stories, mazes, crossword puzzles, and word searches. To minimize time needed for instruction, many games and exercises have been designed as adaptations of ones already familiar to children; preparation time is minimal, usually 10 minutes or less.

Most exercises are for the class as a whole. Generally, individual worksheet activities function as optional activities or as follow-up reinforcements.

Materials needed are minimal and inexpensive. Most are available in school stockrooms, e.g., paper, posterboard, index cards, or markers. A culmination activity, answers to puzzles and a list of on-line library catalogs are included in separate appendixes for easy reference.

The contents of this book are divided into "information to share" passages, denoted with a dialog bubble; activities, indicated with a hand icon; and worksheets.

 information to share   **activities**

Activity and Information Sharing Sequences by Grade Level

Games and exercises in this book can be used independently to teach single concepts or in combination to develop complete library skill sets. In the latter case, the authors recommend these sequences.

Pre-K		Kindergarten		Grade 1		Grade 2	
p. 9	Who Was Melvil Dewey?	p. 9	Who Was Melvil Dewey?	p. 9	Who Was Melvil Dewey?	p. 9	Who Was Melvil Dewey?
p. 10	Fiction or Nonfiction?	p. 10	Fiction or Nonfiction?	p. 10	Fiction or Nonfiction?	p. 10	Fiction or Nonfiction?
p. 10	Musical Library	p. 10	Musical Library	p. 10	Musical Library	p. 10	Musical Library
p. 11	20 Questions	p. 11	20 Questions	p. 11	20 Questions	p. 11	20 Questions
p. 12	While the Librarian is Away…	p. 12	While the Librarian is Away…	p. 12	While the Librarian is Away…	p. 12	While the Librarian is Away…
p. 20	Dewey Decimal Classification	p. 18	Where Will You Find Animals?	p. 17	Three Flowers Worksheet	p. 17	Three Flowers Worksheet
p. 21	Create a DDC Bulletin Board	p. 20	Dewey Decimal Classification	p. 18	Where Will You Find Animals?	p. 18	Where Will You Find Animals?
p. 40	Numbers in the Library	p. 21	Create a DDC Bulletin Board	p. 20	Dewey Decimal Classification	p. 19	In the Garden Worksheet
p. 40	Library Pat-a-Cake	p. 40	Numbers in the Library	p. 21	Create a DDC Bulletin Board	p. 20	Dewey Decimal Classification
p. 41	Soap Box Derby	p. 40	Library Pat-a-Cake	p. 40	Numbers in the Library	p. 21	Create a DDC Bulletin Board
		p. 41	Soap Box Derby	p. 41	Soap Box Derby	p. 24	DDC Classification Poster
				p. 49	Making a Book Cover	p. 25	Pass the Hat
				p. 64	Reading a Bookshelf	p. 40	Numbers in the Library
				p. 75	Jump Rope Song	p. 41	Soap Box Derby
						p. 49	Making a Book Cover
						p. 64	Reading a Bookshelf
						p. 75	Jump Rope Song

Laying the Foundation

 ## Who Was Melvil Dewey?

Read the following to all students:

Many, many years ago, shortly before Abraham Lincoln was president of the United States, a man named Melvil Dewey was born in New York. In those days, there weren't very many libraries open to the public. At any early age, he decided that he wanted to change that so that there would be libraries everyone could use. During his long life, he worked hard to make that happen. Also, Mr. Dewey wanted to improve how books were organized in libraries so that people could find them easily, so he invented a system called the Dewey Decimal Classification System (DDC), which is still used today.

Dewey's system for arranging books is used mostly for nonfiction. The main idea of his system is that books about things that are alike should be put on the same shelves so that they are easy to find.

For grades 3–6, continue with:

It was clear to him at an early age that he wanted to bring about important changes in the world. In fact, when he was 16, he bought a pair of cufflinks inscribed with the letter "R," as a constant reminder that his purpose in life was to reform. He dedicated himself lifelong to three areas of change—a practical system for arranging books in libraries, a more simplified system of spelling for the English language, and the adoption of the metric system in the United States. He had limited success with his spelling reform and metric goals, but the basic classification system he devised for libraries in the 1870s, the Dewey Decimal Classification System (DDC), is still used today (with updating) by most public libraries.

In addition to inventing the DDC, Dewey, who was a librarian, also helped found the American Library Association and he published the first library journal. Additionally, he started the first school to train librarians. And while it was Benjamin Franklin who in 1739 founded the first public library in Philadelphia, it was Dewey's work which encouraged the growth of public libraries throughout the country.

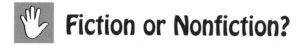 # Fiction or Nonfiction?

Grade Level: PreK–4

Purpose: To help students understand the difference between fiction and non-fiction at a very basic level.

Materials: Books.

Preparation: Collect a selection of fiction and nonfiction books.

Warm-up: Lead a class discussion in which you explain that fiction refers to make-believe or storybooks and that nonfiction refers to books about real people, places, or things.

Game: One by one, hold up some fiction and nonfiction books and ask students to say which they are. Then name the following titles and again ask students if they think the books would be fiction or nonfiction.

> *Mrs. Pig's Day in Court* [made-up]
>
> *What Dinosaurs Ate*
>
> *Rules for Soccer* [made-up]
>
> *The Three Bears*
>
> *Germs Make Me Sick!*
>
> *The Cat and the Hat*

 # Musical Library

Grade Level: PreK–2

Purpose: To understand the concept of books placed in the library by like subjects.

Materials: Laminated individual pictures (animals, musical instruments, and transportation items found on page 12–14); chalk for drawing on blackboard or blacktop; boom box and cassette for music, or a whistle.

Preparation: Using markers or chalk, create three pretend bookshelves: One is for animals; another is for transportation; and the last is for music. These shelves become the "library." Cut out the pictures of the three groups, write "A" for Animals, "T" for Transportation and "I" for instruments on the back of each. Laminate them for durability.

Game: Give one card to each child. Let the children know that by the time the music stops (or other signal is given), they should have taken their pictures to the appropriate area of the "library." Turn on the music. Ask children to take their pictures to their make-believe library and put them in their appropriate "shelves." When the music stops, they compare the letters on the back and see if their cards match with each other (As, Ts, or Is). The area with the most (correct) matching letters wins. If you wish, the music can be turned on again, and children whose cards did not match the others in their area and who think they are in the wrong area have time to move to another area. When the music stops, they check the back of their cards and see if all have correctly ordered themselves in the areas of the library.

Follow-up: Have the children check out books on animals, music, and transportation. Perhaps they could get a book on the item that was in their picture.

 # 20 Questions

Grade Level: PreK–2

Purpose: To understand the concept of classification.

Supplies: Transparencies of picture pages on pages 12–14 (animals, musical instruments, and transportation).

Preparation: Laminate the picture cards if you haven't already for the "Musical Library" game; create transparencies of those picture pages as well.

Warm-up: Show all three pages in succession. Then come back to one of the three and ask what the items on that page have in common. Then go back to the instruments page and ask children what other groups they see on the page (instruments with strings, instruments you hit, instruments you blow). Repeat for the animal page. Elicit responses by asking if all the animals have the same number of legs, etc. Repeat for the transportation page. The goal is to have children name each of the items on the picture pages and tell you something about each to be sure they know their names before you play.

Game:

1. Divide the class into three teams: animal, musical instrument, and transportation.

2. Give four children in a team a laminated card from that grouping. Ask the other members of the team to form around those with cards and help them decide on the correct answer to the other team's questions.

3. Object: To guess the card the player is holding in the fewest number of questions. The team that identifies all of the other team's cards in the fewest number of questions wins.

Round 1:

1. One player on the Animal team looks at his card, and says, "On my card is something from the animal world. Ask questions to guess what it is."

2. Put the transparency of the animal world up on the screen so that the children can see the possible answers and possible groupings.

3. Players from the Instruments Team ask "yes/no" questions one at a time to try to narrow down the category. For example, "Does it have four legs?" or "Is it smaller than a cat?"

4. The child with the picture having consulted with his helpers answers only "Yes" or "No."

5. Questions continue until the animal is guessed. The team gets one point for guessing correctly. You should also record the number of questions asked. If

20 questions are asked before the animal or instrument is identified, the instruments team gets no points. The child holds up the card to show the animal on his card.

Round 2 and Future Rounds:

1. A child from the Instruments team looks at his card and says, "On my card is something from the musical instruments world. Ask me questions to guess what it is."

2. Put up the transparency of the musical instrument world, so players can see the possibilities and formulate questions.

3. Play continues as before with turns passing to the Transportation team and again through the teams until the 12 cards distributed are guessed.

The team identifying the most cards with the fewest number of questions wins.

 # While the Librarian Is Away...

Grade Level: PreK–2

Purpose: To teach the concept of nonfiction books being grouped by like topics. (For grades 1–3, teach the additional idea of nonfiction books being ordered numerically.)

Materials: 8 1/2 x 11" pieces of paper, one per student. One safety pin per student. Cutouts of the cards (one per student) from the "Musical Library" game on page 8 so that there are approximately an equal number of cutouts from the animal, transportation, and instrument groups.

Preparation: Create cards from the "Musical Library" game if you haven't already; affix each card to a sheet of paper for pinning onto clothes.

Warm-up: Prior to playing this game, review "Fiction or Nonfiction?" on page 8 or discuss the fact that fiction books are storybooks and that nonfiction are about real people, places, or things. Add that nonfiction books are grouped on the library shelves by like topics. (Give examples: books on sports are on the same shelf, books on art are grouped together, etc.) Tell them that this game is about nonfiction books, in this case, ones which have to do with animals, musical instruments, and vehicles, like cars, trucks and trains.

Game: Pass out one of the sheets with a card to each child so that there are approximately an equal number of children in each of the three categories. Affix the pictures securely to the students' shirts or dresses with safety pins in a way that the picture is easily visible.

Ask children to form three lines, each line for one of the categories. Select an adult, if possible, to be a librarian the first time the game is played. The librarian will go out of the room while you give the children their directions. (After the children see how the librarian's part is played, one of them can play it in subsequent games.)

With the librarian out of the room, tell the children that they are to pretend they are books in a library, and have them stand straight and tall, shoulder to shoulder. Explain to them that they are very special books. Whenever there is no one around, they come off their shelves and are alive, i.e., the lions roar, the trucks honk, and the flutes toot, etc. The librarian suspects something, because she has heard noises coming from their room, but whenever she checks, they are quietly lined up where they are supposed to be.

Ask the children to note in which line they are standing. When you give a signal, they will begin acting out their animal, vehicle, and instrument roles, as above. However, when you give a second signal, that means that the librarian is coming back to the room. Then all the children will quickly and quietly get back in line "on their shelves" and stand very straight and tall. As soon as they are ready, motion the librarian to come into the room. When she gets there, she will go over and make sure that all the books are in the right lines. She will say, "That's funny. I thought I heard noises in here. Let me see if all my animal books are all on their shelf." She checks and then does the same for the vehicles, and then the instruments If they are in their correct places, she says, "Well, I guess everything is all right. Hmm. I wonder what all those noises were." But if the "books" are not on their correct "shelves," she will say, "A-ha! Just as I suspected. There is something funny about these books. I'll have to keep a better eye on them." Game can be repeated as time permits.

Grades 1–3 Option: The second time the children play the game, write a number underneath their pictures. For example, if there are seven children in the animal group, assign them each a number 1–7, etc. This way, when you signal that the librarian is coming back, the children not only need to get into their proper groups, but also have to be in numerical order, with the smallest numbers on the left, as they would be on a library shelf.

Animal Cards

For activities on pp 8–11.

Musical Instrument Cards

For activities on pp 8–11.

Transportation Cards

For activities on pp 8–11.

Dewey & the Decimals: Learning Games & Activities

Three Flowers

Below are three flowers, each with a theme written in its center. Around the flowers there are words which belong with each flower. Print the words in the petals of the correct flower, crossing them out as you use them. Outline each of the flowers in a different color.

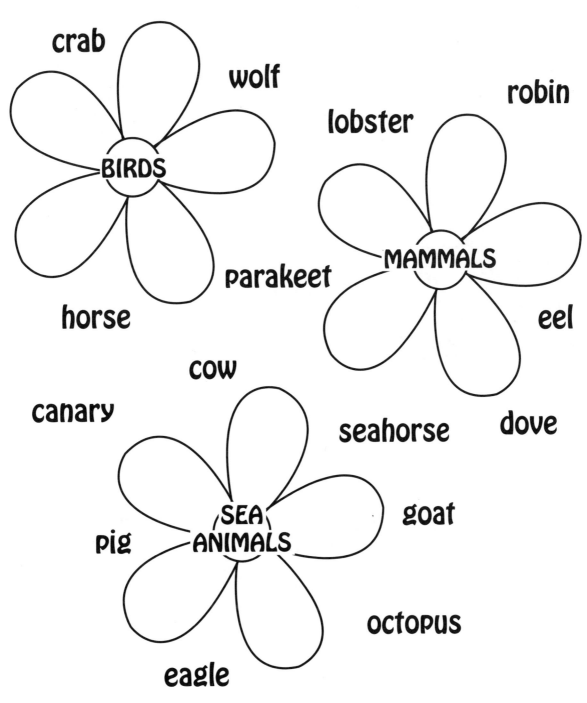

Where Will You Find Animals?

Below are pictures of several animals. Draw a ring around the ones that are wild and a square around the ones that are tame (pets). You will find wild animals in the 500 section of your library and pets in the 600 section.

Follow-up: Go to your library and bring back a book on your favorite pet and one on an animal you'd like to see in the wild.
Share them with your class.

Grades
K–2

Dewey & the Decimals: Learning Games & Activities

In the Garden

1.

Ro__e	P__nsy
L__ly	Vi__le__
Tu__ip	C__rn__tion
D__ffodi__	S__nfl__w____
D__isy	

2.

To__ato	Ca____ot
Tu__nip	Le____uce
__roccoli	Be__n
Bee__	Ra__i__h
Ca____age	

3.

Pea__h	Plu__
Pea__	A__pl__
__a__a__a	Ki__i
Ora__g__	Gr__pe
Li__e	

In the library, books are grouped by themes (what they have in common). Each of the boxes on the left contains words that have something in common. Figure out the theme for each box and write them below:

1. _____

2. _____

3. _____

Then, fill in the missing letters for each word, using your knowledge of that grouping to help you.

Finally, in the last space of each box, write another word that could belong in that group.

Discovering Dewey's System

 ## Dewey Decimal Classification

Read the following to all students:

How do you arrange your books on your shelves at home? By size? Color? Do all your favorite ones go in one place?

What if you were a librarian and had thousands of books to organize so that people could find them easily?

This was the problem that Melvil Dewey began to tackle in the 1870s.

For grades PreK–2, continue with:

When you go to the grocery store, have you noticed that like foods are put on the same shelves? For example, fresh vegetables are in one place, boxes of cereal are in another, and dairy items have their own area too?

Dewey organized library books in similar way, with books on dinosaurs together, books on pets together, and so on. In the games that follow, you will have a chance to do some grouping of your own.

For grades 3–6, continue with:

The system that Dewey devised was for both fiction (books that are make-believe, such as storybooks, novels, science fiction, and mysteries) and nonfiction (books about real places, people, things, and events). Instead of using Dewey's system for fiction, many libraries simply arrange their fiction by authors' last names. However, most use his system for arranging nonfiction books because of the vast amount of books and wide range of topics involved. Briefly, here is Dewey's system for nonfiction:

Nonfiction books are grouped by subject. Each subject has a number between 000–999, and it is printed on the spine of the book. There are 10 main categories (or "classes" of subjects) and 10 divisions in each class. Divisions are then broken down further and decimals can be added to extend numbers for more specific subjects.

 **Create a DDC Bulletin Board**

Grade Level: PreK–6

Purpose: Promote knowledge of and excitement about the Dewey Decimal Classification System.

Materials: Background paper, staplers, photos from magazines representing the classifications, stencils or letters and topical books.

Procedure: Dedicate a bulletin board to the DDC. Each month feature one of the 10 main classes; every week focus on different divisions or topics within that class. *(Example: For "900 — Geography & History," one of the divisions could be Biography.)* See page 22.

Ask children to draw pictures illustrating the featured areas or have them cut out relevant pictures from magazines.

Position a table under the bulletin board. Place library books pertaining to the featured topics on the table. (If this display is in a classroom, encourage students to read books during free time or to write reports on them for extra credit.) If a bulletin board is not available year-round, make a one-time board with representations from all (or several) of the main classes. April is an especially good time for this display, as it is National Library Month.

PreK–3 Option: In one of the drawings or pictures, have children leave out (or cut out) part of the picture. Example: Abraham Lincoln's beard could be missing or Blackbeard could be drawn without his pirate hat. Have children line up and in turn (with a blindfold) pin the missing part on the bulletin board. See who gets closest.

 Dewey About Town: A Story of Dewey in Our World

Grade Level: 4–6

Purpose: Present the DDC in a story format to facilitate understanding of the classifications.

Procedure: Read the following story to students, holding up books or images that correspond to each classification as they appear in the story. Afterward, ask them to try to remember as many of the Dewey Decimal Main Classes as they can. Write their answers on a board or easel, and see if together they can come up with all 10.

Dewey About Town: A Story of Dewey in Our World

Here is a story to help you remember what subject areas each of the Dewey main classes stands for:

Once there was a boy named Asher who was growing up in a small town on the East Coast. One day his father told him that they were moving to a city across the country, because he had been offered a better job. Asher decided to find out more about the new city where they were going. He went to his library, and the librarian helped him find books in the section on General Information.

000s Generalities *(Hold up picture or book.)*

In the city where Asher was moving there lived a girl named Yolanda. She was a daydreamer who liked to spend time thinking about the meaning of life. She was also very interested in people, why they acted the ways they did: why some of her friends were outgoing, while others were shy; why some were easy to get along with, but others were not...in general, "what made them tick." She spent a great deal of time in the Philosophy and Psychology area of her library.

100s Psychology and Philosophy *(Hold up picture or book.)*

When Asher arrived at his new school, he felt very different from everyone else. For one thing, his family was Orthodox Jewish, so Asher always wore a yarmulke on his head. When Yolanda saw Asher, she was very interested in finding out more about him. She asked him about his yarmulke and they talked for awhile about their religious backgrounds and beliefs. They went to their library and found a book on world religions.

200s Religion *(Hold up picture or book.)*

As they continued to talk, Asher told Yolanda about the town he came from and how different this new city seemed. The new city was much larger, more crowded and not nearly as pretty. There was a lot of litter around, and many of the walls and buildings were painted with graffiti. Yolanda suggested that they start thinking about ways to improve their city. They went to the Social Services area of their library and checked out books on urban development.

300s Social Sciences *(Hold up picture or book.)*

One Saturday Yolanda ran into Asher walking home from temple, and she asked him about the book he was carrying. She was unable to read any of the letters she saw on it. "It's in Hebrew," Asher told her. "In my temple the services and readings are all in Hebrew."

"I speak Spanish and a little French," said Yolanda, "but this is the first time I've seen Hebrew. I wonder how many different languages there are in the world."

They continued on to the library and looked up some information in the Languages section.

400s Languages *(Hold up picture or book.)*

Then they began to talk some more about ways they could get ideas for their project from the Sciences area at the library.

500s Natural Sciences *(Hold up picture or book.)*

"And maybe we could bring nature to this city," said Yolanda. "We could plant gardens, build new parks, and clean up the old buildings to make them more attractive. My uncle is an engineer. He could help us draw up the plans, if we make a rough draft." They looked at books in the Technology section to get some clues on how to make blueprints.

600s Applied Sciences *(Hold up picture or book.)*

"And I have another idea," said Asher. "Why don't we cover up some of the graffiti with beautiful murals? Our art teacher said she was once involved in a community mural project, and we could ask her more about it." "And," said Yolanda, "we can look at books in the Arts area of the library."

700s The Arts (Hold up picture or book.)

"And we could add poetry to the murals, too," said Asher. "Let's look under Literature."

800s Literature (Hold up picture or book.)

"I think we also need to look at a map and figure out what streets could most benefit from new gardens and murals," said Asher. "After that, we can read about our city's history," added Yolanda. "That will give us some ideas about themes for our murals." With that they went to the Geography and History area and found several books about their city.

900s Geography and History (Hold up picture or book.)

And that ends our simple story about how Asher met a friend and became a part of his new city. Now, thinking back on the story, see if you can remember the 10 main classes of the Dewey Decimal Classification system.

Option: *To complement the story, create a DDC poster like the sample on the following page.*

DDC 10 Main Classes and Selected Subdivisions

000 – Generalities
020 – Library Science
030 – Encyclopedias
070 – Journalism
090 – Manuscripts & rare books

100 – Philosophy & Religion
150 – Psychology
160 – Logic
170 – Ethics
180 – Philosophy

200 – Religion
280 – Christian denominations
290 – Other religions

300 – Social Sciences
340 – Law
360 – Social problems & services
370 – Education
390 – Customs, etiquette &
    folklore

400 – Languages
420 – English
430 – German
440 – French
450 – Italian
460 – Spanish

500 – Natural Sciences & Math
510 – Mathematics
530 – Physics
580 – Botany
590 – Zoology (wild animals)

600 – Technology
610 – Medicine
620 – Engineering
640 – Home economics
690 – Construction

700 – The Arts
720 – Architecture
730 – Sculpture
740 – Drawing
770 – Photography
780 – Music
790 – Recreation & sports

800 – Literature & Rhetoric
810 – American Literature
820 – English Literature
860 – Spanish & Portuguese
    literature

900 – Geography & History
910 – General geography
920 – Biography
940 – History of Europe
960 – History of Africa

DDC Classification Poster

 # Pass the Hat

Grade Level: 2–4

Purpose: Discover how library books are grouped in the DDC.

Materials: Library books; hat or other container; blackboard and chalk; one sheet of paper per student.

Preparation: Cut out the classification strips below. Place them in a hat or other container. Then pass a hat, and ask each student to take one. If there are more students than strips, some of the students can be assigned the same strip. Have students write down the information on their strips on a big piece of paper so that they won't lose it. You may also wish to make a record of their assignments.

Game Part 1: Ask students to go to check out a book with the numbers they picked, requesting the help of a librarian, parent or sibling if needed. Ask them to choose books from the children's nonfiction section. Ask students to bring in their books the day of the activity, or perhaps the day before, "just in case."

Game Part 2: Write the 10 main Dewey classes on the board, leaving 8–10" of writing space between each class heading. Then call on students individually, asking for the title of their book only. The other students in the class are to guess in which of the 10 categories the book belongs. The student with the book confirms the right answer by looking at the call number of his book and comparing it with the 10 main class numbers on the board. (For example, a book on Hinduism would have a call number in the 290s and so would be in the main class of Religion—200s.) Once confirmed, write the subject of the book on the board under the appropriate general heading. When all of the subjects have been recorded, the class discusses what the books in each category have in common.

Classification Strips

020–029 Library Science	**590–599** Zoology (wild animals)
030–039 Encyclopedia	**610–619** Medicine
070–079 Journalism	**640–649** Home econ., family
150–159 Psychology	**690–699** Buildings
160–169 Logic	**740–749** Drawing
280–289 Christian denomination	**780–789** Music

340–349 Law	**790–799** Recreation & sports
370–379 Education	**810–819** American literature
390–399 Customs, folklore	**820–829** English literature
420–429 English	**860–869** Spanish, Portug. Lit.
440–449 French	**910–919** Geography & Travel
460–469 Spanish, Portuguese	**920–929** Biography
510–519 Mathematics	**960–669** History of Africa
580–589 Botany (plants)	

Memory Match

Grade Level: 3–4

Purpose: To learn and reinforce the 10 Main Dewey Classes.

Materials: Scissors; one set of cards from the following pages for every 2–3 students.

Preparation: Photocopy the following pages of classifications and corresponding numbers. Cut out rectangles along the lines. Laminate for sturdiness and repeated use. Divide class into groups of 2–3 students each.

Game: Have students place all cards face down. One student begins by turning over two cards. If the classification subject matches with the correct corresponding classification number, the player gets to keep the pair and has another turn. If not, both cards are turned face down again and the next player turns over two cards, etc. Play continues until all pairs have been picked up. The object is to match as many pairs of classifications and numbers as possible. The player with the most pairs wins.

Generalities	**000**
Philosophy	**100**
Religion	**200**
Social Sciences	**300**
Language	**400**

Pure Sciences & Mathematics $a+b=c$	**500** $a+b=c$
Technology (Applied Sciences)	**600**
The Arts	**700**
Literature & Rhetoric Poetry	**800** Poetry
Geography & History	**900**

 # Bean Bag Throw

Grade Level: 4–6

Purpose: To develop an understanding of the main classes of the DDC.

Materials: Large piece of poster board, approximately 2' x 2 1/2'; three bean bags (bean-stuffed animals can substitute, the rounder the better); paper for keeping score.

Preparation: Cut five square holes (approximately 5"x5") in the posterboard. Label each category, as below. (*Option:* Around the holes, have students draw small icons representing each DDC class. Examples: pictures of a musical note, paintbrush and a basketball by The Arts, an outline of Africa or a picture of George Washington for Geography & History, etc.)

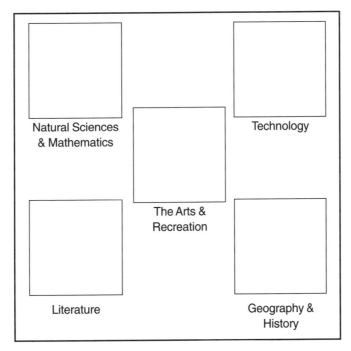

Natural Sciences & Mathematics	Technology
The Arts & Recreation	
Literature	Geography & History

**Bean Bag Throw
Game Board**

Game: Have students line up in front of the posterboard into three approximately equal teams. Suggested distance from posterboard is four to five feet, depending on throwing accuracy of students. Ask one student to hold the posterboard just slightly tilted backward on a chair or low table and to keep it steady while the beanbags are being tossed. At the end of a turn, this student will rotate back into his team's line, and the student who tossed the beanbag will become the next posterboard holder.

Call out a book title from the list below, going back and forth among the five main DDC classes. Each student in turn (alternating teams) names the class in which the book belongs. As she does so, she says why she chose the class, e.g. Major League Bat boy would be about sports, and sports is part of "The Arts." If correct, she then tries to throw the beanbag into the appropriate hole. She gets three tries, if needed. Two points are given for naming the correct division; another point is awarded for getting the beanbag in the correct hole.

Game is played until all students have had at least one turn. The team with the most points at the end of the game wins.

Book Titles for Bean Bag Throw

Natural Sciences and Mathematics

1. *Anno's Mysterious Multiplying Jar*
2. *There's a Wolf in the Classroom*
3. *Where Butterflies Grow*
4. *Watching Desert Wildlife*
5. *Volcanoes*
6. *The Magic School Bus Inside a Beehive*
7. *The Reason for a Flower*

Technology

1. *Mission to the Planets*
2. *The Kids' Book of Chocolate*
3. *A Man on the Moon*
4. *Machines and How They Work*
5. *An Automobile Mechanic*
6. *Incredible Constructions and the People Who Built Them*

The Arts

1. *The Adventures of Three Colors*
2. *Crafts of Mexico*
3. *Duke Ellington: The Piano Prince and His Orchestra*
4. *Fun with Clay*
5. *Chinese Ceramics*
6. *Origami in the Classroom*
7. *Japanese Ink Painting*
8. *Major League Bat Boy*

Literature

1. *Storytelling*
2. *A Light in the Attic*
3. *The Joke-teller's Handbook*
4. *Cowboy Poets and Cowboy Poetry*
5. *Talking to an Audience*
6. *The Vintage Book of African-American Poetry*

Geography and History, including Biographies

1. *We Remember the Holocaust*
2. *Cowboys of the Old West*
3. *Rand McNally Children's Atlas of Native Americans*
4. *Martin Luther King, Jr.: A Man Who Changed Things*
5. *Jesse Jackson and Political Power*
6. *Virginia's General: Robert E. Lee and the Civil War*
7. *Elizabeth Blackwell: First Woman Doctor*
8. *Daniel Boone: Frontier Adventures*

 Library! (Played like Bingo!)

Grade Level: 3–4

Purpose: To become familiar with the 10 main classes and selected divisions of the DDC.

Materials: Scissors and paste for each student; one copy of the next page for yourself and students; a hat or other container.

Preparation: The following page contains the 10 main classes of the DDC (across top of "game board") and 40 selected divisions in the grid below it. The divisions are located directly below their corresponding classes, e.g., Medicine (610) is under Technology (600s). At the bottom of the page are 10 blank rectangles to be used as markers.

Give each student a copy of the next page (game board and grid), and have them cut out the 40 divisions beneath the game board. (Do the same for yourself, and place your cut-up squares in a container.) Have students cut out the 10 blank markers at the bottom of the grid. Students will each select one division per main class and set it in the square directly under the main class. For example, they could put Journalism under Generalities, as in the following:

Sample Bingo square

Game: Have students in turn pick a division from the container, announcing the division and number. As this is done, students who have those divisions on their game boards cover them with markers. The first student to cover all 10 game board squares shouts "Library!" and is the winner.

Short version: The winner is the first student who covers seven squares in a row.

Note: As students become familiar with the divisions and the main classes in which the divisions belong, they can cut off the numbers from their division squares and try to place their squares without the aid of the numbers.

 DDC Bee

Grade Level: 4–6

Purpose: To gain an understanding of selected DDC divisions.

Materials: Chalkboard or easel; a copy of the following page.

Game: Write the 10 main classes of the DDC on board or easel, or post the listing from page 22. Ask the class to line up in two teams. Ask each student in turn, alternating teams, in which main class a division belongs. If a student guesses correctly, he stays standing. If incorrect, he sits down, and the next player in line on the other team tries to answer the same question. After all students have had one turn, the team with the most students still standing wins.

Main Classes

Generalities	Philosophy & Psychology	Religion	Social Sciences	Language	Nat. Sciences & Math	Technology	The Arts	Literature & Rhetoric	Geography & History
000	100	200	300	400	500	600	700	800	900

— GAME BOARD —

LIBRARY!

Divisions

Library Science	Metaphysics	Philosophy & Theory of Religions	Law	English Language	Math	Medicine	Drawing	American Literature in English	General Geography
020	110	210	340	420	510	610	740	810	910
Encyclopedias	Psychology	Bible	Social Problems & Services	German Language	Physics	Engineering	Photography	Literatures of Germanic Languages	Biography
030	150	220	360	430	530	620	770	830	920
Journalism	Logic	Christian Denominations	Education	French Language	Botany	Home Economics	Music	Spanish & Portuguese Literature	History of Europe
070	160	280	370	440	580	640	780	860	940
Manuscripts & Rare Books	Ethics	Other Religions	Customs, Etiquette & Folklore	Spanish Language	Zoology	Construction	Recreation & Sports	Literature of Other Languages	History of Africa
090	170	290	390	460	590	690	790	890	960

— MARKERS —

Dewey & the Decimals: Learning Games & Activities

How Subjects are Broken Down in the DDC

Purpose: To be followed up with the worksheets on pages 34–37.
Dewey was very precise in the way that he organized nonfiction subjects.
Take animals, for example. In Dewey's system, you will find wild animals
in the 500s (Sciences), the care of pets and veterinary services in the 600s
(Technology), drawings of animals in the 700s (The Arts), and animal
trainers in the career section of the 300s (Social Sciences).

Railroad subjects are another example. Books on trains used as
transportation are in the Social Sciences; those on the engineering and
design of trains are in Technology; information on model trains as toys or
hobbies is in the recreation section of The Arts, and books on train stations
can be found in the architecture section of The Arts. Before searching in the
stacks for a book, it's a good idea to look in the library's computer catalog for
the location of the book. The catalog will be discussed in a later chapter.

 # Diamond Dewey Game

Grade Level: 3–6

Purpose: This game is designed to teach and reinforce knowledge of Dewey
classifications.

Materials: Blackboard (for keeping score); 40 index cards, any size

Preparation: On 15 of the index cards, print the number "1." On 12 of them
print "2." On five of them print "3." On three of them print "4." Mix up cards,
then stack them like a deck, numbers facing down.

Set up a small baseball diamond at the front of the class or around the perime-
ter of the room by placing four markers on the floor to serve as bases.

Game: Divide class into two equal teams. Have one team line up. The members
of the other team may stay seated until the first team misses three questions.
Tell the students, "You'll know some of the answers; other times you'll just need
to make a guess. Each student who comes up "to bat" takes the top card off of
the deck and gives it to you. A "1" represents a single, a "2" is a double, a "3" is a
triple, and a "4" is a home run.

Read a question from the set below; if the student answers the question correctly, she gets to take the number of bases shown on the card. If in so doing she
scores a "runner(s)," her team is awarded the according number of points.

Options: (1) If you wish, you can allow the student a specified number of strikes
(missed guesses), depending on skill levels. (2) If there are not three outs by the
time everyone on a team has had a turn, the other team gets to have a turn at
bat.

Diamond Dewey Questions *(correct answers are in italics):*

1. When speaking of libraries, the letters DDC stand for:

a. *Dewey Decimal Classification* c. Dictionary of Dewey Catalogs
b. Dewey's Carry-out Doughnuts d. none of the above

2. How many main classes are there in the DDC?
   a. *10* c. 5550
   b. 25 d. 100

3. About how many years ago was the DDC devised?
   a. 10 c. *125*
   b. 50 d. 400

4. The DDC is used by most libraries for:
   a. all fiction c. mysteries only
   b. reference books only d. *all nonfiction*

5. Which one of the following books would be considered nonfiction?
   a. Lightfoot the Elephant c. A Light in the Attic
   b. *The First Light Bulb [bogus]* d. Lighten Up, Louise [bogus]

6. What type of book cannot be checked out of a library?
   a. *reference book* c. science fiction
   b. books 25 or more years old d. paperbacks

7. How did Dewey spell his first name?
   a. Melville c. *Melvil*
   b. Mellville d. none of the above

8. What is the other major classification system used in the United States besides the DDC?
   a. Library of New York system c. Ames Alphabetics system
   b. *Library of Congress System* d. Dickens' Decimal system

9. Books on cooking would fall under:
   a. *Technology* c. The Arts
   b. Science d. None of the above

10. Books on sports are in the same main class as:
    a. magic c. photography
    b. sculpture d. *all of the above*

11. True or false, mysteries belong in the nonfiction section in the Literature (800s) area. *(Answer: false.)*

12. In addition to devising the DDC, Dewey dedicated his life to:
    a. scuba diving c. birdwatching
    b. *free libraries for everyone* d. playing his flute

13. Books on law can be found which Main Class?
    a. *Social Sciences* c. Literature
    b. Technology d. The Arts

14. Books on mythology are located with:
    a. *books on religion* c. books on the Greek language
    b. books on folklore d. books on Roman history

15. Books on rap music are in which of the following Main Classes?
    a. *The Arts* c. Literature
    b. Social Sciences d. none of the above

16. A children's cookbook would be shelved in:

a. Fiction

b. *Technology in nonfiction*

c. The Arts

d. it can only be bought in a bookstore

17. Books on the German Language would be found in:

a.Technology

b. The Arts

c. Geography and History

d. *None of the above*

18. You would find a book on how to take care of dogs in

a. Natural Sciences

b. *Technology*

c. Generalities

d. Languages

19. True or false, only adults are allowed to use books from the reference section. *(Answer: false.)*

20. A book about the Vietnam War would be found in

a. *Geography and History*

b. Generalities

c. Languages

d. None of the above

21. Most encyclopedias are found:

a. *in the Reference Section*

b. behind the Reference Desk

c. in Fiction

d. with the magazines

22. True or false: Books on Botany, which is the study of plants, can be found in the Natural Sciences section of the library. *(Answer: True.)*

23. True or false: It is all right to check out a book from the reference section if you have had no library fines for 2 years and you have your parents' permission. *(Answer: False.)*

24. Mathematics books are located in the same DDC main class as:

a. *Natural Sciences*

b. Technology

c. Generalities

d. The Arts

25. Books on family problems would be found in which main class?

a. *Social Sciences*

b. The Arts

c. Generalities

d. Technology

26. Books on castle architecture would be found in:

a. Natural Sciences

b. *The Arts*

c. Generalities

d. Literature

27. Shel Silverstein's *A Light in the Attic* would be found in:

a. *Literature*

b. The Arts

c. Fiction

d. None of the above

28. A book on traveling in France would be found in:

a. Languages

b. The Arts

c. *Geography and History*

d. None of the above

29. A book on libraries would be found in:

a. The Arts

b. *Generalities*

c. Natural Sciences and Math

d. None of the above

30. True or false, all nonfiction books on animals are found in the same main class. *(Answer: False.)*

Crossword: The Arts (700s)

The answers to this puzzle are topics of books found in The Arts (700) section of the library. Complete the puzzle using the clues below.

Across

1. Motion pictures shown in theaters
3. The art of making pictures using colored liquids
5. The art of designing buildings
6. Activities played for fun, such as cards, tic-tac-toe, or Simon Says
7. Various art projects made with one's hands, such as paper cutouts

Down

1. Sound made when singing or playing instruments
2. Three-dimensional art shaped usually from marble, metal, wood or stone
3. Pictures made using a camera
4. A type of story acted on stage
8. Activities or games requiring physical effort, such as baseball or soccer

Grades
4–6

Word Unscramble: 790-799s

Unscramble the following words, which have a common theme. Can you figure out what the theme is? Hint: You will find books on the topics scrambled below between 790 and 799 in the library.

1. CERCOS   __ __ __ __ __ __

2. LBSTKAAELB   __ __ __ __ __ __ __ __ __ __

3. TOLBFALO   __ __ __ __ __ __ __ __

4. NTESIN   __ __ __ __ __ __

5. ELBSALAB   __ __ __ __ __ __ __ __

6. MGSIWNMI   __ __ __ __ __ __ __ __

7. YEHCOK   __ __ __ __ __ __

8. SHIFGNI   __ __ __ __ __ __ __

9. ISRUFGN   __ __ __ __ __ __ __

The theme for the above topics is _____.

Word Search: Literature (800s)

One of Dewey's goals was to devise a standard way of arranging books in libraries. Another goal? Find the answer in the puzzle on this page.

The following book topics are found in the 800 (Literature) section of Nonfiction:

1. ESSAYS   2. PLAYS   3. POETRY   4. WRITING
5. HUMOR   6. PUBLIC SPEAKING.

Find these words in the puzzle and circle them. (They may go forward, backward, up or down, but not diagonally.) Cross out the words you have circled, then cross out all Qs, Xs and Zs. Write the remaining letters in order (left to right) in the spaces at the bottom of the page to find the answer.

```
G  N  I  K  A  E  P  S  C  I  L  B  U  P
H  E  W  A  Q  Y  R  T  E  O  P  S  N  T
H  E  D  T  H  Z  E  R  X  E  T  Y  O  B
U  Q  E  F  R  E  Z  E  L  I  B  A  R  X
M  S  Y  A  S  S  E  A  R  I  E  L  S  Q
O  F  G  N  I  T  I  R  W  O  R  P  X  E
R  V  E  Q  R  Y  Z  X  O  Q  N  Z  E  X
```

One of Melvil Dewey's goals: __ __   __ __ __ __ __ __

__ __ __ __ __   __ __   __ __   __ __ __ __

__ __ __ __ __ __ __ __   __ __ __

__ __ __ __ __ __ __ __ .

Grades
3–6

Dewey & the Decimals: Learning Games & Activities

Putting Biographies in Order

All About Biographies

- Biographies are books about the lives of famous people.

- Autobiographies are written by people about themselves.

- Collective Biographies are books about two or more famous people.

- In most libraries all three types of biographies are shelved in the 920s, because real people's lives are part of history (900s). In some libraries, however, biographies do not have their own special section. Rather, they are mixed in with the rest of nonfiction according to subject; for example, a book about Babe Ruth would be located with books on sports in the 700s.

- Biographies about individuals (as opposed to collective biographies about two or more people) sometimes have their call numbers shortened to 92 (from a 920s number). However, they are still located in the 920s area. The 92 or 920s number is usually followed by the last name of the person being featured in the book and the first 3 letters of the author's last name. (This policy may vary slightly from library to library; some libraries only use the first initial of the author's last name.)

- Biographies are arranged alphabetically by last name of the person featured in the book, not by author.

The following is a list of biographies and their authors. Using the information provided above, number them 1–6 in the order in which they should appear on the bookshelf.

_____ *Pablo Cassals: Cellist of Conscience*, by Jim Hargrove.

_____ *Gloria Estefan*, by Rebecca Stefoff

_____ *Bill Cosby: America's Most Famous Father*, by James Haskins

_____ *Sammy Sosa, Home Run Hero*, by Jeff Savage

_____ *Lucille Ball: Pioneer of Comedy*, by Katherine E. Krohn

_____ *Woodrow Wilson: Visionary of Peace*, by James T. Rogers

Grades
3–6

Putting Numbers in Order

 ## Numbers in the Library

Read to grade PreK–2 students: In the DDC, nonfiction books are placed on library shelves by number. In order to find a book, you need to know two things: the book's number and how to place numbers in order. The activities in this chapter give you practice in counting and ordering numbers.

Read to grade 3–6 students: In the Dewey system books are ordered with 3-digit numbers from 000-999. Some subjects are further divided into more specific topics by adding numbers to the right of a decimal. Here is an example: Books on pets are all given 636 numbers, with books on dogs having a specific number of 636.7. The activities in the chapter give you practice in ordering numbers with decimals.

 ## Library "Pat-a-Cake"

Grade Level: PreK–K

Purpose: To teach young children that books in a library are arranged in a special order.

Materials: None

Game: Have children pair off and face partners. Go over the words below with them two or three times, then say the words out loud as they clap a pat-a-cake pattern. On each beat indicated with a "/," they will clap alternating hands with their partners, and on "Xs" they will clap their own hands together.

   /   x   /   x / x /   (x)
I've got something to share with you.

   / x / x   /   x / (x)
I'm a librarian, and here's what I do:

    /   x   / x
I put books in order—1,2,3 *(on "1,2,3" children raise 1, then 2, then 3 fingers)*

  / x   / x
Or by their authors, A–Z *(on "A–Z" children draw an "A" and a "Z" in the air)*

   /   x   /   x / x / (x)
Want to know more? Then just ask me,

  /   x / x / / /
When you visit my li-brar-y! *(on "li-brar-y" children clap both hands with partner)*

 # Soap Box Derby

Grade Level: PreK–2

Purpose: To learn to put numbers in ascending order

Materials: 10 4x6" cards, numbered 0–9 and 10 cards, numbered 000–999 (by hundreds); One set each of cut-out soap box derby numbered cars 0–9 and 000–900; 10 books.

Preparation: Photocopy enlargements of the soap box derby car for each child and write in the appropriate number with just the first numeral of each three-digit number highlighted. (See pattern on page 40.)

Warm-up Activities for PreK–K:

Help children count, 0–9. Explain that they need to include "0", because this is a game to get them ready for library skills, and libraries have a "0s" area in their bookshelves. If they have difficulty counting, try some of these activities:

a. Count books or other objects with the children and put the number in front of the pile of books so that the relationship between the number of books and the written number is clear.

b. Sing a number song like "This Old Man."

c. Show a number chart with numbers matched to pictures of books, e.g. "5" shows five books next to it.

d. Share a counting book or two such as *Anno's Counting Book* by Mitsumasa Anno, *One Crow: A Counting Rhyme* by Ruth Young, *Ten, Nine, Eight* by Molly Bang, *Zoe's Sheep* by Rose Brusik, *My Very First Book of Numbers* by Eric Carle, *Winnie-the-Pooh's 1 2 3* by A. A. Milne, *The Balancing Act: A Counting Song* by Merle Peek and *Count* by Denise Fleming (1–10, 20–50). On the Internet, you could show the children *Bip the Frog* counting book that counts aloud with music 1–10.
http://www.ozemail.com.au/~woodelf/bip1.html

e. Point to the numerals on the number chart and have students call out the number with you.

f. Ask one child to come forward. Ask the child to hold up the number card showing how many students are standing in front of the room. Call up another student, and ask them to select the right number card. Continue until there are nine children at the front of the room.

Derby for PreK–K:

Ask 10 students to come forward. Hand out the 0–9 cars in a mixed-up order. (***Option:*** Allow them to trace their numbers in a marker of their choice.) When you say, "Line Up!" they are to line up on the starting line (point out a line) in order 0–9 (left to right), showing them where "0" will be. Time them.

After they have finished, ask another 10 children to come up and do the same. See if they can do it faster than the first group.

Warm-up for Grades 1–2:

If students are not able to count to a 100, you may wish to share *Count and See (1–100)* by Tana Hoban. They will also need to be able to count by 100s, starting with 0 and going to 900. Once they are able to do so, place 10 large cards 000–900 on a chalkboard railing, ground, or write numbers by hundreds 000–900 on the board.

Derby for Grades 1–2:

Distribute cut-out derby cars 000–900 to children and ask them to trace the numbers with marker colors of their choice. Have 10 of them come to the front of the class at a time. Tell them to order themselves from 000 to 900 as quickly as possible when you say "Line Up!" Time them. When they are finished, bring another 10 forward and see if they can beat the time.

Option for Grades 1–2:

Explain to students that nonfiction books are placed in the library on book-shelves, with numbers ranging from 000 to 999. Ask students to write down a number of their choice between 000 and 999 on a blank card. Suggest that they are books, and that they need to go to the bookshelf where they belong. When you say "Line Up!" have them line up in front of the appropriate hundreds card on the chalk railing or floor. Then review the DDC chart on page 22, pointing out each number's Dewey classification.

Soap Box Derby Car Pattern

 # Decimal Ordering

Grade Level: 3–4

Purpose: To learn the basics of putting decimal numbers in order.

Materials: One copy of the worksheet below for each student.

Read to students: Now you are going to learn about the numbers that fall in between 1, 2, 3, 4. One way of expressing these numbers is through fractions, such as "one-third," "one-half," etc. Another way is through "decimals," pronounced "des-i-mals." A decimal is a dot, like a period. When you say a number with a decimal out loud, you call the decimal a "point."

Write on the board and say:

1.1 One point one
2.4 Two point four
3.5 Three point five

Photocopy the rest of this page for reinforcement:

. . . .

Decimal Ordering

Place a decimal, or dot, in between the paired numbers below.
The first one is done for you. Say the numbers to yourself.

1 . 1	1__6
1__2	1__7
1__3	1__8
1__4	1__9
1__5	2__0

Notice that 2.0 comes after 1.9, just as twenty comes after nineteen. However, most of the time 2.0 is written just as 2, since it does not need a decimal.

Below are three series of numbers, reading downward.
Place the missing numbers in the spaces.

2.0	2.7	4.4
2.1	2.8	4.5
2.2	2.9	4.6
___	___	___
2.4	3.1	4.8
2.5	3.2	4.9
___	___	___

Fox and Chickens

Grade Level: 3–4

Purpose: To reinforce basic decimal concepts (to one significant digit only).

Materials: Slips of paper, one per student.

Warm-up: Help students practice counting out loud as a group starting with 0.1, 0.2. 0.3 etc., to 4.0. (It is helpful to say the zeroes when first learning the numbers, then drop them later after they learn the concept.) Visual learners may find it easiest if you write the first few numbers on the board. When students are able to count to 4.0, they are ready for this game.

Preparation: Determine the number of students who will be participating in the game. You will need slips of paper with decimal numbers on them, as many slips as there are students in the class (minus one). The numbers will start with .1 (it may be helpful to say 0.1 to get started) and go upwards in increments of one tenth.

Game: All of the students except one stand in a large circle facing inward. These are the "chickens." One student, "the fox," stands in the middle. Place the slips of paper in a hat or other container. Have the fox pick one. Only he and you know the number on the paper. One designated chicken will start by saying "0.1." Going clockwise, the next chicken will say "0.2," etc. When a chicken says the number the fox is holding, the fox chases after that chicken. The chicken runs around the circle and tries to get back to her original position before the fox tags her. If the fox catches her she is the next fox. If not, choose a new fox.

Game option: Lead all the chickens in counting together "0.1, 0.2, 0.3, etc." When they get to the fox's number, the fox chases after any chicken he wishes, and that chicken becomes the next fox.

Decimal Dynamite

Grade Level: 4–6

Purpose: To reinforce decimal ordering concepts.

Materials: One unlined sheet of 8 1/2 x 11" paper per student.

Game: Divide students into teams of about 7–10 players, with equal numbers on each team. (It is easiest if there is a distance of several feet between teams.) Choose a team captain or have teams choose one.

Players on each team form a line. Hand each team member an 8 1/2 x 11" paper with a large printed number containing a decimal (see examples below), each team having the same set of numbers. (At this point players are only allowed to look at their own papers.)

When you say "Go," team players hold up their papers at chest height, numbers facing out, so other players on the same team can see them. The teams then order themselves according to their numbers, small to large. When the team is in numerical order, the leader raises her hand. The first team to accurately order themselves wins.

Game option: The captain is responsible for ordering players on her team, rather than all the team players organizing themselves.

Suggested decimal numbers to be assigned to individual students, based on teams of 10 players:

Grade 4: 2.2, 2.8, 4.1, 4.8, 4.9, 7.3, 10.1, 10.5. 11.2, 11.8.

Grade 5: 1.28, 1.82, 1. 92, 2.31, 2.34, 2.43, 2.46, 3.01,3.1, 3.63

Grade 6: 2.005, 2.052, 2.205, 2.25, 2.502, 5.002, 5.02, 5.022, 5.123, 5.213

 # "Who Is It?" Worksheet and Class Discussion

Grade Level: 3–6

Purpose: Understand the "controversial" books classification.

Procedure for Grades 3–4: Complete the "Who Is It?" worksheet on the next page. Then, read the text below to explain.

Read to Students Grades 3–6: In the Scottish Highlands there is a very deep lake called Loch Ness. ("Loch" is the Scottish word for "lake.") Many people say they have seen a monster in this lake, and they have given her the nickname of "Nessie." Some say that she has a long neck like a giraffe with small horns on her head; others say she has humps like a camel, and there are still others who claim that she is over 40 feet long and has flippers like a seal.

Does the Loch Ness Monster really exist? No one has been able to prove it, and some "evidence" has been shown to be a hoax. Since Nessie is "controversial," books about her have been put in the 001.9 area of the library along with other controversial topics. Can you think of some other subjects you would find in the same section?

Note: Some possible answers would be UFOs, flying saucers, Abominable Snowman or Pyramid Power.

If Nessie's existence is ever disproved, books on the Loch Ness Monster might be placed in the 300s area with books on folklore.

Who Is It?

Connect the stars to find out who is in the picture.

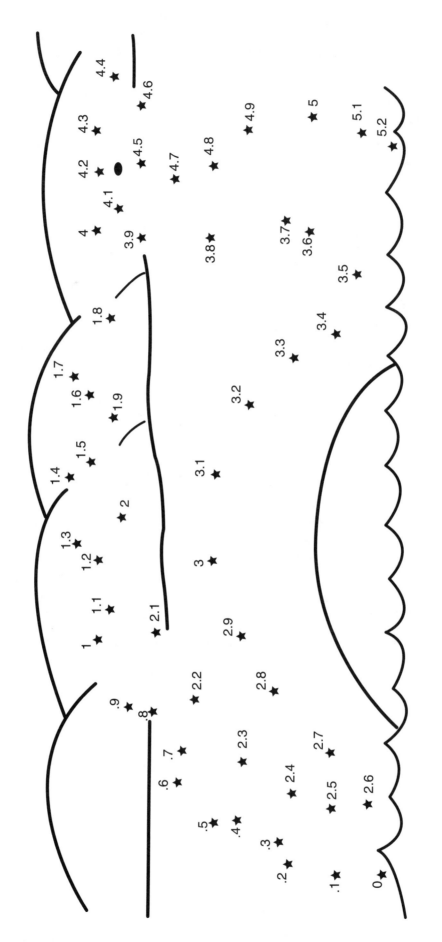

Is it a dinosaur? No… Is it a dragon? No… It's _____

Practice with Decimals

Below are lists of decimals, which need to be placed in order, starting with the lowest number at the top. Choose your skill level and then write the decimals in their correct order (1–10) in the blanks to the right of each series.

Skill Level 1	Skill Level 2	Skill Level 3
429. 1 _____	711.11 _____	928.001 _____
533.9 _____	711.01 _____	928.0101 _____
333.5 _____	701.11 _____	928.101 _____
849.4 _____	700.01 _____	928.19 _____
952.1 _____	700.11 _____	928.023 _____
651.8 _____	710.11 _____	928.03 _____
241.2 _____	710.01 _____	928.031 _____
182.5 _____	710.07 _____	928.0031 _____
041.3 _____	710.77 _____	928.213 _____
711.1 _____	717.01 _____	928.312 _____

Call Numbers

 ## Key Concepts

- Each nonfiction book in the library has a call number, which is like an address. It tells where the book is located in the library.

- Call numbers are a combination of numbers and letters. In the Dewey system, the numbers range from 000–999.

- The letters are generally the first three letters of the author's last name, although some libraries only use the first letter.

- Biography call numbers have a special format.

- Sometimes before the numbers there are special letters which give further information about the book's location. For example, "R" stands for reference, and "J" stands for juvenile.

- Call numbers for audio or visual materials have the same numbers as books, i.e., a book and a video about pets would both have Dewey numbers of 632. (See "Special Letters" on page 59.)

 ## What is the Library of Congress?

The Library of Congress is the largest library in the world. Just how large? It consists of three huge buildings which have a total of more than 17 million books, with about 7,000 being added each day. In fact, together the three buildings have over 532 miles of bookshelves!

The catalogers at the Library of Congress are responsible for developing and updating both the DDC and the Library of Congress systems. They then distribute the information to libraries throughout the United States and many parts of the world.

 ## DDC vs. LC Call Numbers

Libraries generally use either the Dewey Decimal Classification (DDC) system or the Library of Congress (LC) system for arranging books. In the

United States, most public libraries use the DDC, and the majority of colleges and universities use the Library of Congress, but there are many exceptions, with each library (or library network) choosing the system which better meets its needs.

The following are the major differences between the DDC and LC systems:

- The DDC categorizes books into 10 general areas using a numbers system from 000–999. It then subdivides its categories further, using decimals when needed. Finally, it adds letters from the authors' last names for further identification.

- The LC system is based on 20 general areas, each designated by a letter. It sometimes, but not always, adds a second letter for subdivisions. Further breakdowns are made by adding on numbers 1–9999, plus some additional letters and/or numbers.

The final number/letter combinations for both systems are "call numbers."

Write the four call numbers listed below and say: The following are call numbers from the DDC and LC systems. Which do you think are DDC call numbers? LC call numbers?

790.1 OAK
Z253.U69
E169.I.H6
612.84 PAR

(Answer: The first and last are DDC numbers; the middle two are from the LC system.)

 ## Making a Book Cover

Grade Level: 1–3

Purpose: To learn the parts of a book cover, including call numbers.

Materials: One photocopy of the book cover template; a list of titles, call numbers, etc. for students to place on the book cover template, in the form of strips; thick construction paper, with fold marks indicated; crayons or markers.

Warm-up: Review the parts of a book cover with the children, using a nonfiction book the children know well: (title, author, cover art, spine, Dewey number). You might do the following: ask one student to come forward to help; hold up several books that are familiar to the class, one at a time; for each book, ask the class, "What's the title?" Have the student at the front of the class point to the title (both on the cover and on the spine.) Ask, "Which is bigger—the title on the cover or the title on the spine?" Bring another student forward and repeat practice with author, author's last name (both on the spine and on the front cover), and description. Explain "call number." (You might say, for example, if you want to call someone on the telephone, you need to know the telephone number. If you want to find a book in the library, you need to know the call number. Libraries organize books in sections by call numbers just as the grocery story organizes food in sections by type.

Book Cover Procedure:

1. Cut the strips of book information apart.

2. Give each child the information for one nonfiction book.

3. Ask the child to read the title (or read the title to the child); continue with author and the Dewey call number.

4. Ask each child to imagine what the book is about and to draw cover art that would make others want to read the book.

5. Ask each child to cut out the author, title, (big text for the cover and small text for the spine) and the Dewey number from the strip and paste it on their book cover in the appropriate places.

6. Last, ask each child to point to the author, title, and call number on the spine of his book.

Sample Book Cover Strips

Title	Author	Last name	Description	Call Number
Bigfoot and Other Legendary Creatures	Paul Robert Walker	Walker	Explores the myths and scientific questions about such legendary creatures as the Loch Ness monster, Bigfoot and the Yeti	001.944 WAL
Growing Up Amish	Richard Ammon	Ammon	Photographs, maps and drawings show the homes, work and schooling of an Amish community in the late 1800s and early 1900s	289.7 AMM
The Story of Money	Betsy Maestro	Maestro	A history of money from the barter system used in ancient times to the first use of coins and paper money, to the development of modern monetary systems	332.4 MAE

Book Cover Template

Title

Author's Name

FOLD HERE

Title

Call Number

FOLD HERE

Description

💬 Building Call Numbers

According to the Dewey Decimal Classification System, every book, whether fiction or nonfiction, can be given a classification number, also called a "call number." Most libraries do not use the Dewey system for fiction. Rather, they place fiction books in a separate area where they are organized alphabetically by the authors' last names. However, some libraries, especially college libraries, file fiction books by their Dewey number. That way the book can be shelved close to the books about the author's life and writings.

The Dewey Decimal numbers are organized by hundreds. That is why every call number has at least three digits, for example, 133, 796, or 973. Each grouping of 100 stands for a different subject area. Books with call numbers in the 700s, for example, are about fine arts and recreation. Books with call numbers in the 900s are about geography and history.

A book about sports would have a call number of 796. Each of the three numbers that form the number 796 also has a meaning, which helps define the exact topic of the book. The "7" in 796 stands for the overall category fine arts and recreation; the "9" stands for recreation (including activities like games, fishing, and horseback riding); and the "6" stands for sports.

To make a call number even more specific we can add decimals to it.

For example, a book about baseball would have a call number of 796.357. The number on the left of the decimal stands for sports and the number on the right of the decimal stands for the specific sport of baseball.

Books about geography and history are shelved in the 900s. A book about the history of the United States would have a call number of 973. The "9" stands for the overall category; the "7" for the continent of North America; and the "3" for the United States. To give a call number to a book about a specific area of United States history, we can add decimals to the main number. The number 973.7, for example, stands for books about the American Civil War.

There is no limit on the number of digits that can appear to the right of the decimal. The more there are, the more specific the subject.

The Nonfiction Bookshelf

DEAR BRONX ZOO	A SNAKE IS TOTALLY TAIL	THE WORLD OF FRESHWATER FISH	FISHES AND THEIR WAYS	WHAT"S IT LIKE TO BE A FISH
J 590.74 ALT	J 591 BAR	J 597 FEG	J 597 HYL	J 597 PFE

Take a look at the bookshelf above. Letter-number combinations at the bottom of the book spines are referred to as "call numbers." The "J" stands for "juvenile," meaning that the book is for children. The numbers to the right of the "J" are from the Dewey system, and the letters underneath are the first three letters of the author's last name. (Sometimes there is room on the spine to print all of the numbers and letters on one line, rather than having the letters underneath the numbers.)

Notice the books are in numerical order, left to right. If two or more books have the same number, they are put in alphabetical order by the authors' last name.

What's Wrong with This Shelf?

The books below were shelved in too much of a hurry, and some are out of order. Write the call numbers in their correct order (going from left to right) in the spaces provided.

FLOWERING PLANTS	STATE TREES	BIGGEST, FASTEST, STRONGEST	LET'S LOOK AT ANIMALS WITHOUT BACKBONES	OUR YARD IS FULL OF BIRDS	SEASHELLS IN ACTION	TROPICAL FOREST ANIMALS
J 582 LEA	J 582 EAR	J 591 JEN	J 592 SEL	J 598 ROC	J 594 NEW	J 599 LAM

_____ _____ _____ _____ _____ _____ _____

Grades
3–6

🖐 Lightnin' Lucy

Grade Level: 3–4; 5–6

Purpose: To practice learning how books are ordered by call numbers.

Materials: Desks or tables; one set of call number strips per player (see pages 53–54). Laminate strips for repeated use.

Object of game: To place strips of paper containing call number information in numerical order (per the Dewey system), as they would be found on a library shelf. If there is just one player, he tries to beat Lightnin' Lucy's record of 20 seconds. If played in small group or as a class, the object is to be the first to win.

Game for one player: Student mixes up the strips on a table. He then times himself to see how long it takes him to put them in order and tries to beat that time in a subsequent attempt. Another student can check his order.

Two or more players: Students each have their own identical set of strips. They mix up the strips for each other. Then when one says "Go," they see who can put the strips in order faster. This game can be played with the whole class; it can also be played non-competitively, with each student pasting the strips in order on another piece of paper.

Lightnin' Lucy Call Number Strips for Grades 3–4

Title	Author	Call Number
Unbuilding	MACAULEY	J 690 MAC
Witcracks	SCHWARTZ	J 817 SCH
The World of Architectural Wonders	CORBISHLEY	J 720 COR
Cathedral	MACAULEY	J 726 MAC
Greek Myths	MCCAUGHEREN	J 292 McC
Machines and How They Work	BURNIE	J 600 BUR
The Earth and How It Works	PARKER	J 550 PAR
The Kid's Diet Cookbook	PAUL	J 641 PAU
Religions Explained	GANERI	J 291 GAN

Lightnin' Lucy Call Number Strips for Grades 5–6

Inside the Zoo Nursery	Trucks	How It Feels to Live with a Physical Disability	Dear Bronx Zoo	Handmade Alphabet	An Automobile Mechanic	Sign Language Talk	No Place to Be: Voices of Homeless Children	The President's Cabinet and How It Works
Smith	Rockwell	Krementz	Altman	Rankin	Florian	Greene	Bereck	Parker
J 590.74 SMI	J 629.225 ROC	J 362.4 KRE	J 590.74 ALT	J 419 RAN	J 629.28 FLO	J 419 GRE	J 362.7 BER	J 353.04 PAR

Reference Area

Most books that are chosen for the reference area of the library are put there because they contain specific facts that many library users might want to know.

One of the jobs of reference librarians is answering questions either face to face in the library or over the phone. Traditionally they have used a collection of reference books that are always in the library to help them answer these questions. Now, many of these questions can be answered without books via the Internet and other computer databases. However, sometimes the fastest way to find a piece of information is just to look in a reference book such as an encyclopedia or dictionary. Other possible reasons for placing a book in the reference section are: 1) It is especially rare or valuable, 2) It is so popular or used so often that one copy is kept in the reference section for use within the library, or 3) It is such a large book with so much information that most people would just want to read a small portion of it or might want to copy a fact or a picture from it.

Can you name some types of books that are frequently placed in the reference section? *(Some possible answers: atlases, dictionaries, encyclopedias, almanacs, collective biographies such as Who's Who in America?, quotation books, etc.)*

Reference books have the same Dewey numbers as the rest of nonfiction. That is, an atlas, which would be found in the 912 section of Geography and History would have a Dewey number of 912 in the Reference section as well. The only difference is that all books in the Reference section have an "R" at the beginning of their call numbers.

Reference Surprise

Grade Level: 4–6

Purpose: To strengthen understanding of the Dewey Decimal System through practice in the Reference section.

Materials: Reference question strips; refreshments.

Preparation: Photocopy the following pages and cut the paper on the dotted lines into strips so that there is one question per strip. Purchase/prepare refreshments.

Procedure: Give each student one strip to research in the reference section. If there are more than 22 students in the class, then more than one student can be assigned the same question. If there are fewer than 22, some students can volunteer to take on an additional question. Each student completes answers, including the reference used and its call number. *Note: Each strip shows one letter of the correct answer, so students will have an idea whether they are on the right track.*

When the class reconvenes, ask students one by one to give their answers and explain why they chose the reference books they did. After confirming the correct answer, ask the student for the letter between the parentheses in the answer. These special letters are then put together in order to read: "We are going to have a party!"

Reference Surprise Questions

. . . . . _ _ _ _ _ . . . .

1. Who said, "I never met a man I didn't like."

(_) _ _ _   _ _ G _ _ _

Reference: _____ Call number _____

. . . .

2. Who was the fifth president of the United States?

_ _ M _ _   _ _ _ _ _ (_)

Reference: _____ Call number _____

. . . .

3. What is the lowest point in North America?

_ _ (_) _ _   _ A _ _ _ _

Reference _____ Call number _____

. . . .

4. What is the highest mountain peak in the world?

_ _.   _ _ _ (_) _ _ T

Reference: _____ Call number _____

. . . .

5. "Our Town" is a play by what author?

_ _ _ _ _ N _ _ _   _ _ _ _ (_) _

Reference _____ Call number _____

. . . .

6. Who wrote the play "Pygmalion"?

(_) _ _ _ _ _   B _ _ _ _ _ _ _   _ _ _ _

Reference _____ Call number _____

7. Who wrote the book *Jane Eyre*?

_ _ A _ _ _ _ _ _   _ _ (_) _ _ _

Reference _____ Call number _____

. . . .

8. World War I ended with what treaty?

The Treaty of __ __ R __ __ (__) __ __ __ __

Reference _____ Call number _____

- -

9. American physicist Edward Teller was born in what country?

__ __ (__) __ __ __ Y

Reference _____ Call number _____

- -

10. Who wrote the song "This Land is Your Land"?

__ O __ __ __ __   (__) __ __ __ __ __ __

Reference _____ Call number _____

- -

11. Who wrote the poem "Captain, My Captain"?

__ __ __ (__)   __ __ I __ __ __ __

Reference _____ Call number _____

- -

12. What small island is southwest of Adelaide, Australia?

__ __ N __ __ __ (__) __ Island

Reference _____ Call number _____

- -

13. "All for one and one for all" was the motto of what group?

__ __ __   __ (__) __ __ E   __ __ __ __ __ __ __ __ __ __

Reference _____ Call number _____

- -

14. Timbuktu is a city in what country?

__ (__) L __

Reference _____ Call number _____

- -

15. What is the name of the artist who painted "Starry, Starry Night"?

(__) __ __ __ __ __ __   __ A __   __ __ __ __

Reference _____ Call number _____

- -

16. In 1995, American composer David Newman wrote the music for what family movie?

   __ __ __   F __ __ __ __ __ __ __ __ (__) __

Reference _____   Call number _____

· ·

17. The Peloponnesian War was fought between Athens and what
    other Greek city-state?

   __ __ (__) __ __ A

Reference _____ Call number _____

· ·

18.   What type of musical is "Porgy and Bess"?

   __ (__) __ R __

Reference _____ Call number _____

· ·

19. What is the capital of Canada?

   __ T __ __ __ (__) .

Reference _____ Call number _____

· ·

20. "Water, water everywhere/Nor any drop to drink" is a line from what
poem?

   __ __ __   (__) __ __ __   __ __   __ __ __

   __ __ __ __ __ __ __   __ A __ __ __ __ __

Reference _____ Call number _____

· ·

21.What kind of animal is a tocu tocu?

   __ O __ __ __ (__)

Reference _____ Call number _____

· ·

22. Who is the author of the book *Crime and Punishment*?

   __ __ __ __ __ __   __ O __ __ __ __ __ __ __ (__)

Reference _____ Call number _____

· ·

Special Letters

Reference books have an "R" at the beginning of their call letters and children's books have a "J" at the beginning of theirs. An "S" or "F" can mean that the book is in another language such as Spanish or French.

Also, some letters tell you that the item is not a book, but instead a video, CD, or cassette. These materials are usually cataloged exactly like books. They have the same Dewey numbers as books (according to subject), but the numbers have a symbol in front of them such as VID, CD or CASS.

Directions: Below is a list of call numbers. Draw a line matching each call number to the correct book description on the right.

Call Number	Book Description
J REF 353 BRO [made-up]	Children's Nonfiction Book Author: Telemann
R 030 JEN [made-up]	Children's Biography Book Author: Symes
VID 292 DUC [made-up]	Adult Nonfiction Author: Teller
92 WOLFE BRO [made-up]	Children's Cassette Author: Dorsette
J 796 TEL [made-up]	Adult Reference Author: Jensen
J 92 LINCOLN SYM [made-up]	Adult Video Author: Duckworth
J CASS 728 DOR [made-up]	Adult Biography Author: Bronson
974 TEL [made-up]	Children's Reference Book Author: Brothers

Grades
3–6

 # What's My Book?

Grade Level: 4–6

Purpose: To reinforce an understanding of call number designations for children's books, adult books, reference books and biographies.

Materials: book title strips; chalkboard; basket or container.

Warm-up: Review the following information prior to the game:

- Reference book call numbers begin with the letter "R."
- Children's book call numbers usually have a letter "J" (for juvenile) before the number.
- Children's reference books are most commonly marked "J REF."
- Adult book call numbers do not have a special letter.
- Biography call numbers begin with "92" (or a number in the 920s)

Write the titles and call numbers from the following page on the board. Ahead of time make one photocopy of the page and cut into strips, one call number/title per strip. Place strips in a basket.

Game: A student is chosen to be "It" and is asked to come up in front of the class. He draws a strip from the basket and looks at it. Instruct the class to guess what the title of the book is by asking "It" only questions with "yes-no" answers. If the student asking the question gets a "yes" response, she gets to take another turn OR guess what the book is. If she does not get a "yes" answer to her question or incorrectly guess the right answer, another student is called on. When a student correctly guesses, she gets to be the next "It."

Instruct the students to use strategy, by asking the following questions: "Is the book written for children?" "Is it written for adults?" "Is it a reference book?" "Is it a biography?" This will help them quickly narrow down the choices.

Note: As students guess the book title, put a checkmark on the board by the incorrect guesses so they can keep track of what has been guessed.

Book Titles/Call Numbers for "What's My Book?" Cut on dotted lines.

. . . .

1. *The Human Body*   R 612 NUM

. . . .

2. *Major League Batboy*   J 796.3 SOL

. . . .

3. *Maple Tree*   582 SEL

. . . .

4. *Ryan White: My Own Story*   J 92 WHI

. . . .

5. *Paul Revere*   J 92 REV

. . . .

6. *I Am Not a Short Adult*   J 203.5 BUR

. . . .

7. *The Macmillan Dictionary for Children*   J REF 423 MAC

. . . .

8. *Famous First Facts*   R 031. KAN

. . . .

9. *Pets of the Presidents*   J 636 CAU

. . . .

10. *The Complete Guide to Checkers*   794 WIS

. . . .

11. *Dictionary of Classical Mythology*   R 292.1303 MAR

. . . .

12. *Melvil Dewey*   92 DEW

. . . .

13. *All I Really Need to Know I Learned from Watching Star Trek*
    158.1 MAR

. . . .

14. *How to Make Elephant Bread*   J 641 MAN

. . . .

15. *The World Almanac*   R 310 WOR

. . . .

16. *Coretta Scott King: Keeper of the Dream*   92 KIN

. . . .

17. *A Deaf Child Listened*   J 92 GAL

. . . .

18. *The Reader's Digest Children's World Atlas*   J REF 912 REA

. . . .

19. *An Actor's Life for Me*   J 92 GIS

. . . .

20. *Libraries and How to Use Them*   J 020 HAR

. . . .

5 Locating Books By Call Numbers

 Reading a Bookshelf

- Usually library bookshelves have labels, which tell the range of book numbers for the shelves, making it easier to find books quickly.

- When looking for a book on the shelves, keep in mind that the numbers read from left to right, and top to bottom. (See below.)

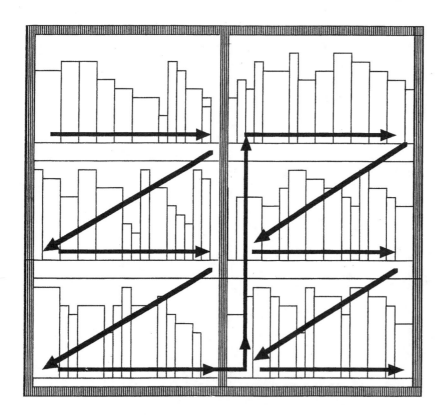

Following the order of books on library shelves is a little like reading a newspaper column. You start at the top left and go right across the shelf; then you go down to the next shelf and go from left to right again. When you get to the bottom, you go up to the top of the next column of shelves.

Mystery of the Lost Lunch Money

Ms. Ortiz took her class to the library for a field trip. While they were there, one of the students dropped his/her lunch money in the nonfiction section in front of the books on European travel. Using the statements and picture below, figure out whose lunch money it is.

- **Lauren** spent her time in the library looking at books on general information and computers.

- **Michiko** looked for books on mythology, then went to find some on raccoons.

- **Gina** thumbed through a book on raising hamsters, then looked through one on building bridges.

- **Jamaal** picked out some biographies, then walked to the shelves on poetry.

- **Nikki** got a book on crafts, then another on painting.

- **Liza** chose a book to read on law, then went to find a Spanish dictionary.

- **Mark** went straight for the books on basketball, then found a book about jazz.

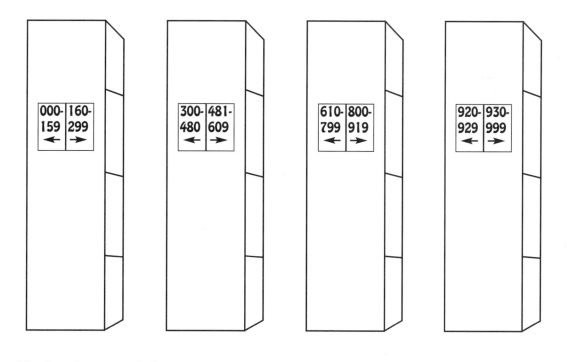

The lunch money belongs to: _____

Hint: If you need help remembering the Dewey Decimal Classification ask the librarian to help you locate a chart showing the main classes and subdivisions.

Grades
4–5

The Shadow: Story and Discussion Questions

Grade Level: 3–4

Purpose: To provide an alternative way to learn about reference materials.

Materials: Reference materials.

Procedure: Read the following story to the class. Afterward, the questions at the end are discussed as a group.

The Shadow

Leah squirmed on the library carpet. She looked at the other kids in her class and wondered if any of them were itching. Then she gazed up at the clock and sighed. Only nine-fifteen.

"Good morning," came a cheerful voice. "I am Mrs. Fitzpatrick, your librarian, and I am going to tell you about the different kinds of books you will find at the library. First, does anyone know the word we use for storybooks?"

Leah was thinking about the question when suddenly a shadow darted across the wall. She rubbed her eyes. The shadow was gone.

"Storybooks are called 'fiction,'" Mrs. Fitzpatrick answered herself. "So what do you think we call the other kind of books, the ones about real things?"

"Un-fiction?" someone asked. The class giggled.

"That's actually pretty close," replied Mrs. Fitzpatrick, smiling to the group. "We call them 'nonfiction'."

Uh-oh. Leah saw the shadow again, but it disappeared as quickly as before. Then she noticed a long thread hanging from the hem of Mrs. Fitzpatrick's skirt. Suddenly something took a swipe at it. She stretched her neck to get a better look. Nothing.

"Dictionaries, encyclopedias, and atlases," Mrs. Fitzpatrick continued. "These are all reference books. They are nonfiction books, which can't be checked out. They stay in the library so that they're always there for everyone to use." Then, she reached over and picked up some items from a nearby table.

"Okay, now we are going to play a game," she announced. "I'm giving each of you a card with the names of three different books to find," she said as she walked among the students.

The children quickly stood up and began to approach the bookshelves. "Hold on," the librarian called after them. "There are a few things you need to know. Fiction books are placed on the shelves in alphabetical order by author's last name, and nonfiction are arranged by their subjects using numbers in the Dewey Decimal System. You will find the authors' last names or the numbers printed on the spines of the book," she said pointing to the spine of a book she was holding.

[Hold up a book and point out the spine]

"Melvil Dewey divided information about the world into 10 areas," Mrs. Fitzpatrick continued. "He then divided each of those big areas into 10 smaller areas, making one hundred areas. He then divided each of the one hundred areas into 10 even smaller areas, making one thousand."

"Each area has a number." Mrs. Fitzpatrick turned around and pointed to the bookcases in the library behind her. "What do you see on the sides of the bookcases?" she asked.

Leah looked and saw the each bookcase had big numbers on the sides. On one she saw 391–459. On another was 600–699. Before Leah could answer, several other children called out, "Numbers."

"What do you think the numbers mean?" prompted Mrs. Fitzpatrick.

Leah's friend Rachel had an idea. "The numbers are like addresses," she suggested.

Sean had an idea, too. "Do they have something to do with the Dewey numbers you were talking about?"

"You're both right," said Mrs. Fitzpatrick. "If you know the Dewey areas, then you know the addresses of all the information in the library. You just go to the area where that information is kept and look for the number. In most libraries there are numbers posted on the ends of the bookshelves, which tell what call numbers are on the shelves. They're sort of like street signs. Well, enough talking, let's get to it!"

Leah looked at her card. First was a reference book. She quickly located the "C" encyclopedia she needed. As she reached down to the lowest shelf to pick it up, she felt something bat her across her left shoulder. She whirled around, but nothing was there.

Her second book was called Tigers and Lions of Africa. [made-up] "That's not a storybook," she thought, "and I already found my reference, so it must be nonfiction." She looked at the list of Dewey numbers Mrs. Fitzpatrick had handed out. She saw that Dewey had a section for information about wild animals: the 590s. She went to the bookcase labeled 460–599 and found that all the books were in order by the number on the spine of the book. She looked at her card again and saw a number next to the title Lions and Tigers of Africa. The number was 599.02. She followed the numbers and found her book on the lowest shelf, but as she reached down to pick it up, the books on the opposite side of the shelf slid off onto the floor.

"Now, how did that happen?" she muttered, as she grudgingly put the books back. "Oh, well," she said, looking at her last card, which was a storybook on birds. "Fiction," she thought, walking towards the children's area. "Author's last name is Miller, so I need to find the "M's." She started to scan the shelves. Suddenly she had a very eerie feeling, and a chill went down her spine. Then, as she stretched to the top shelf to pull down her book, she jumped back and gasped. There were two green eyes staring at her.

Leah laughed. She reached up and lifted down a large gray tabby cat in her arms and went back to where Mrs. Fitzpatrick stood.

"Oh, I forgot to tell you about 'Dui,' our latest addition to the library," said the librarian with a chuckle.

"Can I check him out for two weeks?" teased Leah.

"Now, I ask you, does he look like a book?" Mrs. Fitzpatrick countered.

"Well, he does have a spine, and I can curl up with him on my lap," Leah answered.

"But, alas," said Mrs. Fitzpatrick, "he has the wrong kind of tale."

"Oh," groaned Leah.

> *Cats and libraries have a long history together. Cats were "hired" for many years to keep libraries free of mice, who like to eat the glue on the book bindings.*

Discussion Questions:

1. What is another name for storybooks, that is, books that are make-believe? (Fiction)

2. What do we call books that are about real people, places. or things? (Nonfiction)

3. What do we call books that can't be checked out? (Reference books)

4. How are fiction books arranged in libraries, by authors' last names or by book subjects? (Authors' last names)

5. How are nonfiction books arranged? (Book subjects)

6. Where on a book is its number printed? (Spine) Point out that these numbers are referred to as "call numbers."

Cat Maze

Dui the cat has a special interest in bird watching. He overhears the librarian say that the library has a new book on that topic. Its call number is 598.2 HAR, and it can't be checked out. Help him get through the maze to the area where it's kept.

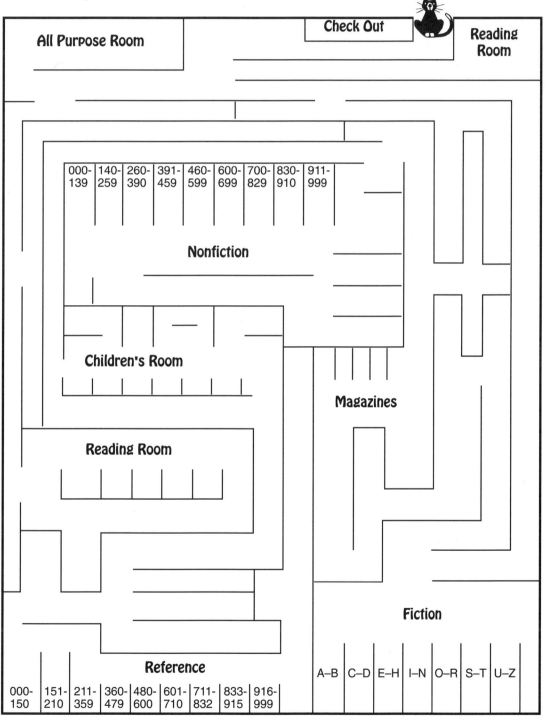

 # Pirate Treasure Hunt

Grade Level: 3–6

Purpose: To give students experience in finding books by call numbers.

Materials for 3–4 grade: Materials for pirate hats and patches: one sheet of black construction paper for hat, and 1/4 sheet of black construction paper for eye patch; scissors, transparent tape, enough string to go around students' heads. (Note: Felt may be substituted for paper to make the patches.) Loot bags—squares of cloth or netting about six inches per side and strings or ribbons for tying them. Loot can be foil-covered chocolate "coins," pennies covered with gold foil, or other treat. Call number slips.

Materials for 5–6 grade: Students in these grade levels may not wish to wear pirate hats and patches, although they might be willing to bring in bandannas. If not, they are still likely to accept some type of loot at the end of their call number trail. Call number slips.

Preparation: Each student makes a pirate hat (or wears a bandanna) and an optional eye patch for the game. (See next page for assembly instructions and templates.) They can label their pirate hat with a famous pirate's name (such as Blackbeard, Anne Bonney, Mary Read, Captain Kidd, Black Bart, Henry Morgan, etc.) or make up their own name. Put loot in the little bags tied with string or ribbon, one bag per team. Teams will consist of three to five players. Create call number slips for a large variety of books in your library. Make sure there is only one book in the library for each of the call numbers you have selected. Hide a bag of loot for each team behind the final books. A good number of call number slips is four books per team.

Game: One set of call number slips will lead participants to books that have call number slips inside, which will lead them to more books with slips inside and so-on. When they pull the final book off the shelf, they will find the hidden loot behind it. If you would like this to be a competitive game, the first team to find their loot is declared the winners.

Read the following to students to start off the game: "Ahoy, there, Mateys! Put on your pirate hats, bandannas, and patches, and prepare for a treasure hunt. Someone has hidden bundles of loot in the library stacks, and it's up to you to find the loot.

"But first, a little about pirates: They have been in existence for about as long as people have been sailing the seas, but about 500 years ago they were a major force in the world when they attacked and stole from explorers bringing home treasures from the New World. Perhaps the most famous of them were Captain Kidd, Black Bart, and Blackbeard, who preyed on ships in the 1600s and 1700s.

"Here's a question: In which Dewey Main Class do you think you would find information on pirates?" *(Review the 10 classes, if needed. Answer: 900s, because pirates are a part of history.)*

Hat Assembly Instructions

1. Photocopy the pirate hat template at 115% onto stiff paper for tracing.

2. Fold 8 1/2 x 11" black construction paper in half horizontally.

3. Trace pattern on one side of folded paper, extending sides to reach the edge of the page.

4. Cut out pattern on all sides. You will now have two pieces.

5. Tape sides together, adjusting to fit the child's head. If needed, you can add extender strips between sections.

6. Have child write their favorite pirate's name on white paper, cut it out and glue it to the front of the hat.

Patch Assembly Instructions

1. Photocopy the patch template onto stiff paper for tracing.

2. Trace template on black construction paper and cut out.

3. Fold patch in half as indicated over a length of string and tape the string ends together.

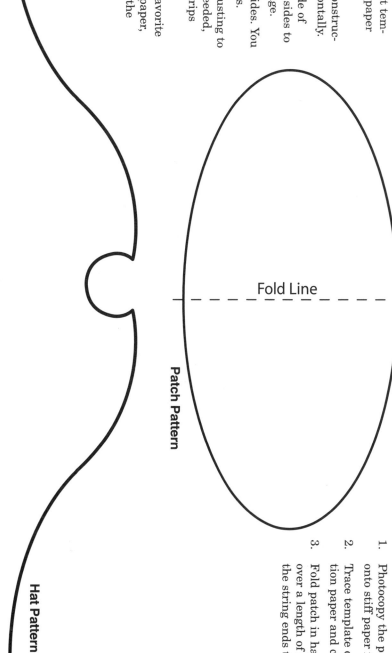

pirate name

Fold Line

Patch Pattern

Hat Pattern

Computer & On-line Catalogs

 ## Background Information

Before computers, books in libraries were located using card catalogs. Usually in the center of a library's main reading room, alphabetized cards were kept in wooden or metal drawers and a reader could look up a book by title, author, or subject. Large libraries had hundreds, even thousands of these drawers. Every time a book was added or subtracted from the library's collection, cards had to be added or taken out. It was an extremely time-consuming process, not to mention a waste of trees!

Today, library catalogs are computerized. Now it is a very simple matter to add or subtract catalog records from the database. Now there are many more ways to search for a book using computer catalogs. One can search by title, author, or subject. One can also use any words from the title, author, or subject. This is called "key word" searching. It is very useful when you can't remember the exact title or author. It also works well when you want to find several books on a certain topic. Computerized catalogs not only have more ways to search for an item, but they also give you a lot more information than the old card catalogs could. They can tell you which branches of the library own the book and whether it is on the shelf or checked out. On many systems, you can even place a hold on a book and tell the computer to which branch you would like the book sent for check-out.

Often a library's computer catalog can be viewed from your home computer by logging onto the library's Internet website. Here you can not only use the catalog but can find out lots of information about library programs, library hours and directions to the library. You may also place a hold on a book right from your home computer. You can check on how many items you currently have checked out and see whether any of them are overdue. Many library websites offer links to other useful websites that you might use for a homework assignment or a hobby. Some libraries even offer electronic books that you can check out and read right on your home computer screen!

Why Use the Computer Catalog?

It's not always easy to find the best book to answer your question just by using the Dewey number. Let's say you wanted to find a book about Hercules, a hero of Greek mythology. What Dewey number would you look under? Probably in the 200s (religion, including mythology), right?

How many books do you think your library has in the 200s section?

The Los Angeles Public Library has over 3000 books in the 200s.

A keyword search for "Hercules" shows more than 165 books, but not all of them are about the myth of Hercules. Some are about an aircraft called the Hercules and others are about Hercules in art or music or film.

It would take quite a bit of time to find a book about Hercules if you had to search through hundreds or even thousands of books on the shelves, and Hercules' name might not even be mentioned in the title, so you'd have to open every book about Greek mythology and read the table of contents or the index to see if Hercules was mentioned.

With a computer catalog, you can actually type in the keywords "Hercules mythology" and read a list of the mythology books the library has about Hercules. In the Los Angeles Public Library that's only 35–40 books. Some of these are in the 200s, but others are in other sections of the library.

Let's say you wanted to find a book about the history of baseball in Cuba. Would you go to the numbers for sports, for history, or for Cuba? A quick search of the library computer catalog with the keywords "baseball history Cuba" would instantly tell you the exact books you could go to on the shelves. It wouldn't matter if one library shelved the same book under sports, while another put it under history; your computer catalog search would give you the Dewey call number, and you could easily find the book on the shelf.

With the computer catalog, you can find the information you want quickly. You can find books by author, subject, title, keyword, or call number.

Also, in most cases, the computer will show you the status of the book (whether it's checked out or not). It may even show you books that your library does not have, but that it can get from a nearby library. Often you can place a hold on the book and have it brought to your library in two or three days, just by clicking on the right screens on the computer.

Library Word Search

Can you find the following Dewey and library words in the puzzle below?
(Words can go forward, backward, up or down, but not diagonally.)

ATLAS   CLASSIFICATION   FICTION
AUTHOR   DECIMAL   REFERENCE
BIOGRAPHY   DEWEY   STACKS
CALL NUMBER   DICTIONARY   SUBJECT
CATALOG   ENCYCLOPEDIA   TITLE

R S E S T A C K S C B R D T T E
U A F I C T I O N A B P I F I C
K L L A C D T O T T A R C C T N
Z T A T D E C I M A L Q T B L E
R A M V Q W B M I L J P I Y E R
O S U B J E C T B O Q P O A F E
H I C L U Y Z R A G N L N E A F
T Y H P A R G O I B O A A E B E
U R D R W E N E G Z I E R X U R
A I D E P O L C Y C N E Y I U A
C A L L N U M B E R R T V A S Z
O N O I T A C I F I S S A L C V

Dewey & the Decimals: Learning Games & Activities

Jump Rope Song

Grade Level: 1–4

Purpose: Reinforce the concepts of the computer catalog and call numbers.

Materials: Long jump rope.

How Many Books?

I went to the library yesterday

To check out books on a Shakespeare play.

I got my call numbers from the catalog

On the computer, then ziggity-zog

I headed *straight* straight* straight* for the stacks,

Loaded up my arms clear up to the max.

How many books did I get?

Check...them...out!
(Twirlers speed up and count 1, 2, 3, 4, 5, 6, 7, etc. until jumper misses.)

 # On-line Catalogs—How Do You Use Them?

Grade Level: 3–6

Purpose: Give students a guided tour of their library's computer catalog.

Materials: One photocopy per student of the following page, "Searching the On-line Catalog" with the library's URL written in the blank.

Warm-up: Explain to the students that each library makes its own web page, and each one looks a little different. Each one, however, will have the word "catalog" somewhere on it. They'll want to find "catalog" and click on it with the mouse. They can search for a book by title, author, subject, or keyword.

Searching the On-line Catalog

Using an Internet browser on your computer, such as Netscape or Internet Explorer, type in the address (or URL) for your library: _____

In a keyword search, you might even use special search terms to be sure you find the books you want:

- To make sure you only find books you can read, you can add "juvenile" to your search terms. Then only books intended for young people will be found.

- Once you've searched by subject and found the Dewey call number that fits what you're looking for, use the first three numbers of the call number as a search term. Then you can read the description of each book in that call number on the computer before going to the shelves.

- You can even search to find a book on tape or a video by using the search terms "audio" or "video."

When you enter your search terms, remember:

- Put the word or phrase you are searching on in quotes.

- Capitalization usually doesn't matter (***Example:*** *you can enter California or california*)

- Names of people must be entered with last name first (***Example:*** *White, Nancy*)

- Hyphenations usually don't matter (***Example:*** *"trade-in" or "trade in"*)

- Punctuation usually doesn't matter (***Example:*** *"biology a study in modern science" or "biology: a study in modern science" give the same result.*)

Search Type	Example of What to Enter	Search Results
Title (title list or title browse)	The first part of the title. ***Example: "Baseball in"***	An alphabetical list of titles that begin with ***"Baseball in"***
Author (author list or author browse)	The author's last name (if it's a common name you might use last name, first name). ***Example: "White, Nancy"***	A list of titles by authors whose names begin with ***"White"***
Subject (Subject list)	A word that tells what the book is about. ***Example: "baseball"***	An alphabetical list of titles about baseball, broken down into smaller categories like ***"Baseball: coaching"*** and ***"Baseball: history"***
Keyword (or Power Search or Advanced Search)	A word or words from any part of the book listing. ***Example: "White and stars and bus"***	A list of titles that contain all three key words: ***"The Magic School Bus Sees Stars*** by Nancy White"
Dewey Decimal Call Number	A call number	A list of titles with call numbers close to the call number you entered

Grades 3–6

Dewey & the Decimals: Learning Games & Activities

Boolean Searching on the Internet

There is an amazing amount of information to be found using the books in the library or sites on the Internet. The information we are looking for can be tracked down much more quickly in the library or on the Internet by using "Boolean" searching. Most library computer catalog keyword searches and most Internet search engines allow Boolean searching. Some search engines only use the Boolean search terms in their advanced search. Some library computer catalogs automatically search for "and," so it is not necessary to type the Boolean operator between keywords. Read the searching directions on your library catalog website to be sure.

Boolean searching is named after the English mathematician George Boole, born in 1815. Boole was a largely self-taught mathematician who founded a new field of mathematics called symbolic logic. For many years Boole's ideas were interesting only to philosophers and mathematicians, but today we all use his ideas. They influenced the design of computer circuits and telephone switching as well as computer catalog and Internet searching techniques.

Let's say you wanted to find out information about tigers either in the library or on the Internet. In the library, you'd use the computer catalog to find your information. On the Internet you'd use a search engine. On the Internet search engine "Google," the search term "tiger" produces a list of 1,670,000 websites that have the word tiger in them. At the Houston Public Library, the catalog lists more than 660 books on tigers. The Los Angeles Public Library catalog lists nearly 1,200 books on tigers. You cannot possibly look through all of those books or all of those websites to find the information you need.

To narrow your search so that you'll have a reasonable number of websites to examine, you'll need to use the Boolean search terms "and," "or" and "not." These terms let you limit your search to only the information that you want.

Let's say you mainly want to know where tigers live and what they eat and you want to make sure you don't get information on Tiger Woods or Tony the Tiger. You can ask the search engine to search for tiger *and* habitat *and* diet *and not* Tony *and not* Woods.

With these Boolean search terms, Google lists only 2,300 sites (with the sites that match all the terms first); The Los Angeles Public Library lists only a handful of books on tiger AND habitat. The Houston Public Library catalog lists less than 10 books on tiger AND habitat.

It will certainly be easier to look at those few books and focused websites than the hundreds, or thousands, or millions there are when the only search term we use is "tiger." Thank you, Mr. Boole!

Note: Distribute the following page to each student and read aloud.

Search Terms with Boolean Operators

You can search broadly by putting in just one search term such as baseball. You can narrow your search by asking the computer only to look for books that have two search terms. Connect the terms using "*and*." For example: "baseball AND history." You can narrow it even more by adding a third keyword: "baseball AND history AND Cuba."

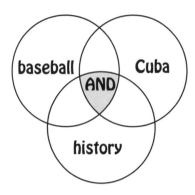

You can narrow your search by typing "*not*." For example, if you want information about baseball but *not* about its history, you can type "baseball NOT history."

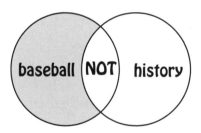

You can broaden your search by linking two search terms with the word "*or*." For example, you might try "photographs OR camera OR pictures."

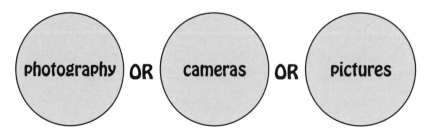

What Is Spoken Here?

Complete the puzzle below about languages spoken around the world.

- Find the country in which the city is located by using a world atlas in the 912 area of the Reference section. Write the name of country next to the city.

- Go to the computer catalog (or the Internet) and find a book about each country in the puzzle. Look up the language of that country. Write that language in the crossword.

- Write the call number of the reference book in the parentheses next to the appropriate puzzle clue.

Across

Languages spoken in:

1. Alessandria, _____
   (_____)

4. Essen, _____ (_____)

6. Nagoya, _____ (_____)

7. Aleksandrov, _____ (_____)

8. Dar es Salaam, _____ (_____)

9. Le Mans, _____ (_____)

Down

Languages spoken in:

2. Lorca, _____ (_____)

3. Eilat, _____ (_____)

5. Maidstone, _____ (_____)

Grades
4–6

Dewey On-line Scavenger Hunt

Grade Level: 4–6

Purpose: Provide experience locating books in the computer catalog by author, title, keyword, subject, and call number.

Materials: At least one computer connected with Internet and/or library catalog access.

Warm-up:

- Introduce children to the function of the computer catalog (see pages 70–71).

- Go to the catalog search screen for your library or for a major library in your area (see Appendix C).

- Demonstrate the use of a search screen using a projected computer screen, if possible.

Scavenger Hunt: Have students complete the Scavenger Hunt Chart and answer the Challenge Questions. The first to do so correctly wins. Have them use the following websites (also listed at the bottom of the chart):

Houston Public Library: *http://www.hpl.lib.tx.us/hpl/index.html*
Los Angeles Public Library: *http://www.lapl.org*
Seattle Public Library: *http://www.spl.lib.wa.us*

Note: Some websites, including the one for the Seattle Public Library, require the use of a browser that can be Java-enabled, such as Internet Explorer or Netscape. Most likely your browser is already Java-enabled, but if it is not, follow these steps:

Internet Explorer

Click on the Edit menu. Click "Preferences." Select "Web Browser," then "Java." Select "Enable Java" so that a check mark appears at the selection. Close "Preferences."

Netscape

Click on Edit menu. Click "Preferences." Click "Advanced." Check the boxes "Enable Java" and "Enable Java Script." Close "Preferences."

Title	Author's Last Name	Author's First Name	Description	Call Number Houston Pub. Lib.	Call Number Seattle Pub. Lib.	Call Number L.A. Pub. Lib.
1. Breaking Into Print: Before and After the Invention of the Printing Press	Krensky	Stephen	Describes books before the printing press was invented and discusses the effect of that invention on civilization.	686.2 K		x085 K92
2. Truth About Unicorns	Giblin	James Cross	Describes the animals that inspired the tales of the unicorn and tells myths about it from around the world.		J398.2454 Giblin	x133 G446
3. The Book of Think: Or, How to Solve a Problem Twice Your Size		Marilyn	Easy-to-follow guide to analytical thinking and problem solving skills with clear and interesting examples.	153.4 B	J153.43	x153 B967
4. The Story of Religion	Maestro		Introduces the history of religious belief and explores the practice of religion in the world today.	291 M	J291 Maestro	x290 M186
5.	Krementz	Jill	Tells the stories of 12 children with various types of disabilities including blindness, paralysis, and cerebral palsy.	362.4 K	J362.4083 Krementz	x362.8209 K92
6. Internet	Koehler	Lora	Explains in word and pictures what the information superhighway is and how it can be used.	004.67 K		x384.6K77
7. Many Luscious Lollipops: A Book about Adjectives	Heller	Ruth	Introduces adjectives and their uses through brief rhyming text.	425 H477	J425 Heller	x425 H477
8.	Cobb	Vicki	Tells how to make fruit drinks, grape jelly, muffins, chop suey and yogurt while demonstrating scientific ideas.	507.8 C	J507.8 Cobb	x500 C653-8

Scavenger Hunt Chart

Title	Author's Last Name	Author's First Name	Description	Call Number Houston Pub. Lib.	Call Number Seattle Pub. Lib.	Call Number L.A. Pub. Lib.
9. *Blood and Guts: A Working Guide to Your Own Insides*	Allison	Linda	Discusses the parts of the human body and includes suggestions for related experiments.	612 A438	J612 Allison	
10. *Arms and Armor*	Byam	Michelle	The story, in pictures and words, of hand weapons and armor from the Stone Age to the Wild West.		J355.8241 Byam	x623. B993
11. *On the Brink of Extinction: The California Condor*	Arnold	Caroline	Describes the history of the condor in North America and the efforts to save it from extinction.	598.912 A		x639 A752
12. *Draw 50 Dinosaurs and Other Prehistoric Animals*		Lee	Provides step-by-step instructions for drawing different dinosaurs and other prehistoric animals.	741 A	J743.6 Ames	x743 A513
13. *Sweet Words so Brave: The Story of African American Literature*	Curry	Barbara K.	Presents a short history of African Americans and their literature.	810.9 C	J810.98960 Curry	
14.	Bauer	Marion Dane	Tips for writing fiction with ideas on character, plot, point of view, dialogue, endings and revising.	808.31 B	J808.1 Bauer	x809.3 B34
15. *Mummies Made in Egypt*	Aliki	(none)	Tells how and why mummies were made in ancient Egypt.	932 A411		x932 A411

Use the following websites in your Scavenger Hunt:

Houston Public Library: *http://www.hpl.lib.tx.us/hpl/index.html*
Los Angeles Public Library: *http://www.lapl.org*
Seattle Public Library: *http://www.spl.lib.wa.us*

Dewey & the Decimals: Learning Games & Activities

Dewey On-line Scavenger Hunt Challenge Questions

Be the first to return with correct answers to these questions. You may need to ask your librarian for help, but try to think of the answer yourself first.

1. Why does Seattle put Krensky's book in the 600s while Houston and Los Angeles put it in the 0–99 Dewey numbers?

2. Why is the Truth about Unicorns kept in the 300s by Seattle but in the 100s by Houston and Los Angeles?

3. Why is Lora Koehler's book in the 0–99 section in Seattle, but in the 300s in Los Angeles and Houston?

4. Why is Arms and Armor in the 300s in Seattle but in the 600s in Los Angeles and Houston?

5. How many books does the Seattle Public Library have about baseball? (***Hint:*** *be sure to search by "topic key words."*)

6. How many books does the Seattle Public Library have about the history of baseball? (***Hint:*** *be sure to search by "topic key words."*)

7. How many books does the Seattle Public Library have about the history of baseball in Cuba? (***Hint:*** *be sure to search by "topic key words."*)

Grades
4–6

Appendix A

●●●●●●●●●●●●●●●●●●●●●●●●●●●●●●●●●●

Culmination Game

Dewey Want to Be a Millionaire?

Grade Level: 4–6

Purpose: To reinforce an understanding of concepts connected with Dewey classifications, call numbers, locating books and catalogs.

Preparation: Prior to playing the game, students should have been exposed to all the information in this book. Having previously played the games designated for grades 4–6 is also an asset. Photocopy onto light green paper one set of "Dewey Dollars" per team. (See page 86 for patterns.)

Materials: Chalkboard or other device for keeping score. "Dewey Dollars."

Game: Divide students into teams of four to five. There are enough quiz questions for seven teams. Time limits can be set, if needed.

- A spokesperson is chosen for each team.

- Only one team is on the "hot seat" at a time, but other classmates may be involved as part of "help lines."

- If a team is not sure of an answer, they are allowed to use one "help line" during their round. Their options are (1) polling their classmates as a whole, (2) polling another team or (3) asking that two of the multiple choice answers be eliminated.

- To give other members of the class an incentive in assisting with the "help lines," the class as a whole gets points for every team that makes it through Level #4.

- Ask the team that is "up" a question from Level #1. The team discusses the question among themselves, and the spokesperson is required to give an answer. (If the team cannot agree on an answer, it is up to the spokesperson to make the final decision.) If the team is correct, they are awarded a $10 Dewey-dollar bill, and they proceed to a question from Level #2. If they answer that question correctly, they are given a $1,000 Dewey-dollar bill, and move to a question from Level #3. If correct, they are awarded a $100,000 Dewey-dollar bill, and they go to the last question, which is from Level #4. If correct, they win a $1,000,000 Dewey-dollar bill.

- If a team misses any questions along the way, the next team gets a turn.

- Dewey-dollar bills and points from assisting via the help line can be turned in for privileges such as free time, reduced homework and extra credit.

Option: If the class would like to play additional rounds, have them make up questions for the other teams.

Dewey Want to be a Millionaire—Questions *(correct answers are in italics):*

Level 1:

1. The first name of the inventor of the Dewey Decimal system was:

   a. Mervyn

   b. Melvin

   c. *Melvil*

   d. Malavai

2. Before computers, cataloging information about library materials was put on what?

   a. papyrus

   b. *index cards*

   c. cash register tape

   d. tissue paper

3. Melvil Dewey, inventor of the Dewey Decimal Classification system, was a:

   a. mathematician

   b. logician

   c. *librarian*

   d. dentist

4. When you have tried to find information at the library on your own, but are not successful, you should:

   a. call 911

   b. give up and go out for ice cream

   c. *ask a librarian*

   d. hope you can find someone in your class who found the answer

5. A call number is:

   a. the catalog phone number

   b. a library's after-hours number

   c. *a number on the spine of a book*

   d. a prime number

6. The computer catalog is the same as

   a. The Internet

   b. Websites

   c. an e-mail system

   d. *none of the above*

7. Books on which subject would **not** be shelved next to the others?

   a. *cartoons*

   b. trucks

   c. motorcycles

   d. cars

Level 2:

1. Books with lots of maps would most likely be found in which section of the library?

   a. 600s

   b. 700s

   c. 800s

   d. *900s*

2. Books about the planet Neptune would be found in which section of the library?

   a. 300s

   b. 400s

   c. *500s*

   d. 600s

3. The Library of Congress is located in which city?

   a. Philadelphia, PA

   b. Boston, MA

   c. *Washington, D.C.*

   d. Sacramento, CA

4. Who started the first public library in the United States?

    a. George Washington   c. *Benjamin Franklin*
    b. Bill Gates   d. Melvil Dewey

5. Where was this first public library established?

    a. New York   c. Richmond, VA
    b. Washington, D.C.   d. *Philadelphia, PA*

6. Which library has the greatest number of books?

    a. The New York Public Library   c. *The Library of Congress*
    b. The Los Angeles Public Library   d. The Kalamazoo Public Library

7. In the DDC, call numbers range from:

    a. 000–10,000   c. 1–100
    b. *000–999*   d. 1–10

Level 3:

1. Books on which subject would ***not*** be shelved next to the others?

    a. tigers   c. elephants
    b. lions   d. *dogs*

2. Which is ***not*** a common way to search for books in an online catalog?

    a. by title   c. by keyword
    b. by author   d. *by publisher*

3. Books on which subject would ***not*** be shelved next to the others?

    a. snakes   c. iguanas
    b. lizards   d. *squirrels*

4. Books on which subject would ***not*** be shelved next to the other?

    a. corn   c. *hamburgers*
    b. tomatoes   d. squash

5. A call number of 92 means that the book is a:

    a. reference book   c. *biography*
    b. mystery   d. novel

6. An autobiography is a book which:

    a. was printed off the Internet   c. a book about a famous car
       by an automated system

    b. *a book written by a person about*   d. none of the above
       him / herself

7. A cataloger determines:

    a. the price of a book   c. *call number of a book*
    b. the size of a book   d. how many pages a book should be
       have.

Level 4:

1. Books on which subject would *not* be shelved near the others?

   a. poetry

   b. *advertising*

   c. essays

   d. drama

2. Books on which subject would *not* be shelved near the others?

   a. chemistry

   b. *philosophy*

   c. physics

   d. biology

3. Books on which subject would *not* be shelved near the others?

   a. *cooking*

   b. fishing

   c. swimming

   d. horseback riding

4. A book on public speaking would be found in which area?

   a. social sciences

   b. *literature and rhetoric*

   c. the arts

   d. technology

5. The call number "PE1628.5W4" belongs to which system of library classification:

   a. Dewey Decimal

   b. *Library of Congress*

   c. it could belong to either

   d. it does not belong to either

6. If you type the words "customs and Russia" to do a Boolean search, you will get information on:

   a. *Russian customs only*

   b. everything that has to do with either customs OR Russia

   c. you will get an error message

   d. none of the above

7. Which book would be on the most specific subject?

   a. 632

   b. 632.2

   c. 632.24

   d. *632.245*

Dewey Dollars

Appendix B

●●●●●●●●●●●●●●●●●●●●●●●●●●●●●●●

Answers to Games and Worksheets

Chapter 1: Laying the Foundation

Page 15 **Three Flowers** Sea Animals—crab, octopus, seahorse, eel, lobster; Birds—
dove, canary, eagle, parakeet, robin; Mammals—goat, pig, wolf, cow, horse.

Page 17 **In the Garden** Flowers—rose, pansy, lily, violet, tulip, carnation,
daffodil, sunflower, daisy; Vegetables—tomato, carrot, turnip, lettuce, broccoli, bean,
beet, radish, cabbage; Fruit—peach, plum , grape, lime, lemon, orange, apple, kiwi,
banana.

Chapter 2: Discovering Dewey's System

Page 34 **Crossword: The Arts (700s)** Across—movies, painting, architecture, games,
crafts; Down—music, sculpture, photography, drama, sports.

Page 35 **Word Unscramble: 790–799s** 1.soccer; 2. basketball; 3. football;
4. tennis; 5. baseball; 6. swimming; 7. hockey; 8. fishing; 9. surfing.
Theme—Sports.

Page 36 **Word Search: Literature (800s)** Dewey's goal: He wanted free libraries for
everyone.

Page 37 **Putting Biographies in Order** *Lucille Ball: Pioneer of Comedy, Pablo
Cassals: Man of Conscience, Bill Cosby : America's Most Famous Father; Sammy
Sosa:Home Run Hero; Woodrow Wilson: Visionary of Peace.*

Chapter 3: Putting the Numbers in Order

Page 45 **Practice with Decimals** Skill Level 1—041.3, 182.5, 241.2, 333.5, 429.1,
533.9, 651.8, 711.1, 849.9, 952.1; Skill Level 2—700.01, 700.11, 701.11, 710.01,
710.11, 710.07, 710.77, 711.01, 711.11, 717.01; Skill Level 3—928.001, 928.0031,
928.0101, 928.023, 928.03, 928.031, 928.101, 928.19, 928.213, 928.312.

Chapter 4: Call Numbers

Page 51 **The Nonfiction Bookshelf** Order of call numbers—J 582 EAR,
J 582 LEA, J 591 JEN, J 592 SEL, J 594 NEW, J598 ROC, J 599 LAM

Page 52 **Lightnin' Lucy** Grades 3–4—J 291 GAN, J 292 McC, J 550 PAR,
J 600 BUR, J 690 MAC, J 720 COR, J 726 MAC, J 817 SCH;

Grades 5–6—J 353.04, J362.4 KRE, J362.7 BER, J419 GRE, J419 RAN, J 590.74 ALT J590.74 SMI, J 629.225 ROC, J629.28 FLO.

Page 55 **Reference Surprise** 1. (W)ILL ROGERS; 2. JAMES MONRO(E); 3. DE(A)TH VALLEY; 4. MT. EVE(R)EST; 5. THORNTON WILD(E)R; 6. (G)EORGE BERNARD SHAW; 7. CHARLOTTE BR(O)NTE; 8. VERSA(I)LLES; 9. HU(N)GARY; 10. WOODIE (G)UTHRIE; 11. WAL(T) WHITMAN; 12. KANGAR(O)O; 13. THE T(H)REE MUSKATEERS; 14. M(A)LI; 15. (V)INCENT VAN GOGH; 16. THE FLINTSTON(E)S; 17. SP(A)RTA; 18. O(P)ERA; 19. OTTAW(A); 20. THE (R)IME OF THE ANCIENT MARINER; 21. RODEN(T); 22. FEODOR DOSTOYESVK(Y)

Chapter 5: Locating Books by Call Numbers

Page 63 **Mystery of the Lost Lunch Money** The lunch money belongs to Jamaal.

Chapter 6: Computer & On-line Catalogs

Page 77 **What is Spoken Here?** Across—1. Alessandria, Italy (Italian); 4. Essen, Germany (German); 6. Nagoya, Japan (Japanese); 7. Aleksandrov, Russia (Russian); 8. Dar es Salaam, Tanzania (Swahili); 9. Le Mans, France (French). Down—2. Lorca, Spain (Spanish); 3. Eilat, Israel (Hebrew); 5. Maidstone, England (English).

Page 79 **Dewey On-line Scavenger Hunt** 1. J686.2 Krensky; 2. 133 G446; 3. Burns; 4. Betsy; 5. *How it Feels to Live with a Physical Disability*; 6. J004.67; 7. [none]; 8. *Science Experiments You Can Eat*; 9. x551 S596-7; 10. 355.8 B; 11. J598.912 Arnold; 12. Ames; 13. x809 C976; 14. *What's Your Story? A Young Person's Guide to Writing Fiction*; 15. J393.30932 Aliki.

Page 81 **Dewey On-line Scavenger Hunt Challenge Questions/Answers**

1. The 600s are the applied sciences and technology, so bookbinding, which is one of the main topics of the Krensky's book puts it in 686.

   Publishing is in the 1–99 section, so that topic for this book causes it to fit nicely in 085.

2. Seattle has grouped the book with other stories about mythical creatures, with fairytales and folktales.

   Los Angeles and Houston have placed the book with other books about strange phenomena and the unknown.

3. Seattle has placed the book in a new section of the Dewey system that deals with computer topics.

   Houston and Los Angeles have the book with others about communication; people use the Internet to communicate.

4. Los Angeles and Houston have placed the book with technology, specifically the applied science of making weapons.

   Seattle has placed the book in a section on military supplies and weapons.

   Since the book deals with how weapons are made, technology is appropriate.

   Since the book also deals with how weapons are used in warfare, grouping it with other books on the military fits well.

5. How many books does the Seattle Public Library have about baseball?

(To be determined at time of activity.)

6. How many books does the Seattle Public Library have about the history of baseball?

(To be determined at time of activity.)

7. How many books does the Seattle Public Library have about the history of baseball in Cuba?

(To be determined at time of activity.)

Appendix C

On-line Library Catalogs

The Internet site at the University of Berkeley provides connections to hundreds of libraries at *http://sunsite.berkeley.edu/Libweb/*

The Las Vegas-Clark County Public Library has links to libraries using the Internet worldwide at *http://sjcpl.lib.in.us//homepage/PublicLibraries/ PubLibSrvsGpherWWW.html*

Here are just a few library catalogs online by area:

The West

Berkeley Public Library, CA
  http://library.berkeley-public.org/screens/opacmenu.html

Los Angeles Public Library, CA
  http://catalog.lapl.org

Oregon Public Library System
  http://www.solis.lib.or.us/PolPac/html_client/

Olympic Peninsula Library System, WA
  http://www.pcl.lib.wa.us/webclient.html

Mountain & Plains States

Denver Public Library, CO
  http://set.coalliance.org:5000/cgi-bin/cw_cgi?getBasicTerms+6825

South Dakota Library System
  http://webpals.sdln.net/webpals/

Coeur d'Alene Public Library, ID
  http://206.63.154.226/athcgi/athweb.pl?a=st

Brigham City Public Library, UT
  http://bcpl.lib.ut.us/wx/s.dll?d=smain

Southwest

Maricopa County Public Library, AZ
  http://mcld.maricopa.gov/web2/tramp2.exe/form/Aold2an6.000

Santa Fe Public Library, NM
  http://catalog.ci.santa-fe.nm.us/screens/opacmenu.html

Midwest and Great Lakes

Bloomington Public Library, IL
http://carlweb.rsa.lib.il.us:1080/cgi-bin/cw_cgi4.3?getBasicTerms+30534

St. Joseph County Public Library, South Bend, IN
http://www.sjcpl.lib.in.us/homepage/online.html

Dayton and Montgomery County Public Library, OH
http://www.dayton.lib.oh.us/

Southeast

District of Columbra Public Library, Washington, DC
http://citycat.dclibrary.org/uhtbin/cgisirsi/VgsaG8BvR7/18949005/60/

Miami-Dade Public Library, FL
http://169.139.19.6/

Charleston County Library, SC
http://www.ccpl.org/marion.html

Northeast

Hartford Public Library, CT
http://caroline.hartfordpl.lib.ct.us/search

Upper Hudson Library System, NY
http://www.uhls.org/web2/tram2.exe/log_in

Newport Public Library, RI
http://204.17.98.73/nptweb.html

Sources

The following list of sources was used when compiling information for this book:

1. Davis, Sydney W. and Gregory R. New. *Abridged 13 Workbook: For Small Libraries Using Dewey Decimal Classification Abridged Edition 13.* Forest Press, 1997.

2. Dewey, Melvil: *Abridged Dewey Decimal Classification and Relative Index, Edition 13.* Forest Press, 1997.

3. Gibbons, Gail. *Pirates: Robbers of the High Seas.* Little, Brown, 1998.

4. Jacobs, James S. and Michael O. Tunnell. *Children's Literature, Briefly.* Prentice Hall, 1996. CD-ROM.

5. *The Library of Congress: 25 Questions Most Frequently Asked by Visitors.* 1997. Pamphlet.

6. Rabinowich, Ellen. *The Loch Ness Monster.* Franklin Watts, 1979.

7. Wiegland, Wayne A. *Irrepressible Reformer: A Biography of Melvil Dewey.* American Library Association, 1996.